The
Complete
Guide
to Writers'
Conferences
and
Workshops

Books by William Noble

Show, Don't Tell, Middlebury, Vermont, 1991

Bookbanning in America, Middlebury, Vermont, 1990

Make That Scene, Middlebury, Vermont, 1988

"Shut Up!" He Explained, Middlebury, Vermont, 1987

Steal This Plot (with June Noble), Middlebury, Vermont, 1985

The Psychiatric Fix (with June Noble), New York, 1981

The Private Me (with June Noble), New York, 1980

How to Live With Other People's Children
(with June Noble), New York, 1978

The Custody Trap (with June Noble), New York, 1975

The
Complete Guide
to Writers'
Conferences and
Workshops

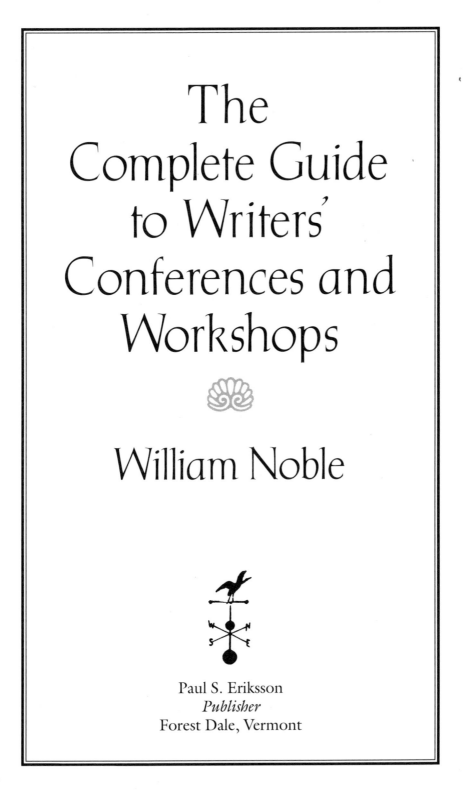

William Noble

Paul S. Eriksson
Publisher
Forest Dale, Vermont

10 9 8 7 6 5 4 3 2 1

Library of Congress Cataloging-in-Publication Data
Noble, William
The complete guide to writers' conferences and workshops / William Noble.
p.   cm.
Includes index.
ISBN 0-8397-1840-3 (pbk.)
1. Authorship — Congresses — United States.
2. Authorship — Congresses — Canada. I. Title.
PN171.6.N63   1995
808'.02 — dc20   95-16108
CIP

Photo Credits: page 21, James Long; page 75, Redlin Photography; page 99, Judy Wandschneider; page 117, Miriam Berkley.

Contents

How To Use This Guide

I T'S NO SECRET we have a plethora of writers' gatherings and groupings, and each has a worthy purpose. But in today's pragmatic world, greater value attaches to writers' conferences and writers' workshops which provide access to professionals who can guide the less experienced through mazes in the writer's art. This *Guide* lists these conferences and workshops, whether they run for one day, two weeks, or periodically over a couple of months. If you're looking for multi-semester, degree-providing writing courses and curricula, you will not find them here. What you will find are short-term writers' gatherings and groupings which offer solid help to those who want to write.

The *Guide* is arranged alphabetically by state and alphabetically by conference or workshop within the state. Canadian entries are arranged alphabetically by conference or workshop title. Each listing includes a detailed summary of the program involved, and, where possible, the words of the sponsors (set in quotes) have been used in the program description. The amount of information should be sufficient so anyone searching *The Guide* will be able to decide—if not on one program, certainly on a narrowed list— where he or she would like to apply. *The Guide* is not intended to duplicate, in full, the information on program brochures or information sheets; it offers a springboard enabling you to pick and choose and contact the programs directly.

Each writers' conference or workshop entry is designed to list the following:

Program—name, address, telephone, fax, description, director/contact, location(s), dates, founding date, enrollment and enrollment limits, scholarships, ancillary activities.

In addition, there are entries for: required manuscripts, editing assistance, individual manuscript conferencing, marketing guidance, attendance by agents/editors, availability of agents/editors for conferencing.

If any of the items on these lists does not appear in the conference or workshop listing, it's because the program did not include it in their information for *The Guide*, or they specifically responded in the negative.

Finally, this *Guide* deals mainly with fiction, nonfiction, and poetry, and no attempt has been made to seek out individual or special opportunities for screenwriting, play writing, film or video writing, unless these are part of a larger conference or workshop that offers fiction, nonfiction, and/or poetry. Then, they are included. The purpose of *The Guide* is to list and describe general writing-learning opportunities through writers' conferences and workshops and to show where they will be and who will run them in throughout the United States and Canada.

Conference and workshop names, addresses, formats, general dates, locations and director/contacts change little from year to year. If a writers' conference or workshop is listed here you can feel confident it will also be offered in subsequent years at about the same time, at the same or similiar place and with the same or similiar approaches to the art of writing.

How We Got Here – A Short History

S OME YEARS AGO, John Ciardi laid out a golden rule for writers and writing: "I do think," Ciardi said, "that there [has been] no writer of any consequence in history who was not at some time a member of a group." Ciardi was speaking from experience, of course; he was a widely published poet and Director of the Breadloaf Writers'Conference at Middlebury College in Vermont [1955-1974]. For him, writers and writers' groups were an unassuming part of history's daily scene. "Every writer I can think of," he went on, "was at one time a member of a group, whether it was the Greek agora, or the Roman bath, or the French café, or the English University."

Through the eighteenth and nineteenth centuries the modern writers' conference—as we know it—was yet to be developed. Cafés, coffeehouses, salons, clubs, were meeting places for writers. Here, of course, the human need to communicate spent itself as it had through the centuries. Better known writers dominated and others were content to listen to them read. Yet writers' groups persisted, even though small and relatively exclusive. Benjamin Franklin was an active member of one, as were Ralph Waldo Emerson and the other transcendentalists. Ideas were discussed, work was presented and somehow the give-take offered enough spark so there would be another crowd at the next meeting.

But a wave of literacy and educational opportunity swept the land after the Civil War, and there were more writers seeking more chances to write. Newspapers and journals proliferated, and by the early twentieth century colleges and universities had expanded their curricula in the study of the English language. In Vermont, Middlebury College had, for some years, been offering summer-school study of foreign languages. Why not use the foreign language model and develop a summer school in English? Make it a Master's level program that called for the study of American and English literature and prepared those who wanted to teach. But don't mix the students with the foreign language students; keep them separate. The truth was that Middlebury owned a money-losing hotel and farm complex at the foot of nearby Bread Loaf Mountain, and putting paying students into the facilities through the summer would add heft to the bottom line.

So the Middlebury Bread Loaf School of English was born in 1920, offering the study of American and English literature and "... teaching methods, public speaking and debate, theory and practice in modern drama and composition." Yet this was not a place for writers to meet with other writers, to read to one another, to learn from one another. These were teachers and scholars going through a formal education process.

But a hint of something special for writers did emerge. If the study of literature could be formalized, what about teaching the *making* of literature, the writing of it? Book publishing and book-writing opportunities were beckoning, and the idea that one could *learn* to write in a school-like setting took hold. Six years later—in 1926—the Bread Loaf Writers' Conference opened, and its debut was the culmination of people like Robert Frost, Willa Cather, Edwin Markham and Katherine Lee Bates teaching at the English Summer School and spreading the word that writers could thrive in the same atmosphere. For years Frost, who summered nearby, had wanted to bring writers together "in a sort of literary camp"; Cather so enjoyed Bread Loaf that she wanted to have a little writing studio there. The idea that *writers* could live and work and teach other writers at Bread Loaf suddenly seemed appropriate.

That first Bread Loaf Conference set a standard that remains a writers' conference baseline to this day. "The program," the initial announcement stated, "will consist of background lectures on the writing of short stories, novels, articles and poems, with practical suggestions on developing a prose style and the preparation and placement of manuscripts." There would be informal discussions and conferences between faculty and students and individual critque sessions which "... should result in marketable writing."

Thirty-five writing students showed up at Bread Loaf that first year, and the faculty was a mix of writers, editors, and teaching professionals. Robert Frost gave a reading, and by the end of the two-week conference, most felt they had a success on their hands. Bread Loaf became an annual two-week event, and Robert Frost, along with other writers and editors, continued regular appearances. But it would be five years before the writers' conference idea surfaced anywhere else. And when it did the location was fifteen hundred miles away from Bread Loaf. In 1931 the first "Conference on Creative Writing" took place at the University of Iowa because Norman Foerster, Director of the University's School of Letters, felt academia was losing out in the development of young writers. He proposed a "school of writing" which would bring together literature and cultural opportunities at the university with the creative skills of the student. Ultimately, his proposal became the degree-granting Iowa Writers Program, but simultaneously, a short-form program blossomed: the Iowa Writers' Workshop under the direction of Paul Engle. Here, people would come for a limited time and throw themselves into concentrated give-take. After the first year, 1931, there was no doubt about its success, and more than forty years later, Eliott Coleman, founding director of the Writing Seminars at Johns Hopkins, could say: "Paul Engle's program became the most extensive and the most famous university writing program in America."

By the mid-1930s, writers' conferences had become entrenched in the summertime cultural consciousness. The University of North Carolina offered one, as did Olivet College in Michigan and the University of New Hampshire. In Boulder, Colorado, the Rocky Mountain Conference, provided this scene to a *Saturday Review of Literature* correspondent: "Newspaper and advertising writers, housewives, school teachers, people with over 200 publications to their credit and people with none heard discussions of poetry, novels, short stories and feature articles; entered into spirited round-table conferences; attended formal lectures by the instructors..."

And by 1940 annual spring issues in both *Publisher's Weekly* and the *Saturday Review of Literature* offered a regular listing of summer writers' conferences, along with a brief discription of the programs. There were still only a handful, however, and each was a creature of a university or college.

The writing spirit, though, is indefatigable, and even the bombing of Pearl Harbor and United States entry into World War II didn't wipe away the writers'-conference experience. In June, 1942 *Publisher's Weekly* could report, "Sumertime writers' conferences and other courses for writers are about to begin, and will be in full swing from the middle of June to the end of August, in various parts of the country." Some programs did cancel, but Highlander Folk School in Monteagle, Tennessee was ready for its fourth annual conference, though it did acknowledge the new reality. "The emphasis will be on writers' opportunities and responsibilities in the war effort," the conference declared. "Pamphlets, leaflets and news stories will be among the subjects of instruction."

By 1945, however, the opportunities for writers to travel and meet were severely curtailed. Wartime restrictions on the use of transportation coupled with a reduced student pool caused many to cancel for the duration. Only Breadloaf and the conferences at the University of New Hampshire and at Northwestern University outside Chicago kept their doors open.

But the resiliency and the value of the writers'-conference idea was underlined in the summer of 1945 when a participant at Northwestern (who also happened to be a war immigrant from Central Europe) could extol the virtues: "If I remember right," he wrote, "there existed no classes in short-story writing, nor any drama work-shops at Central European Universities. Nor did any colleges or high schools publish any magazines edited and written exclusively by students. There was no institution giving us young ones an opportunity of learning the trade and permitting the talented ones to break into print."

And a year later the writers'-conference idea spread once more. *Publisher's Weekly* could report, "There are a few more summer writers' conferences scheduled this summer [1946] than there have been during the war years." But now the opportunities began to move beyond colleges and universities; writers' organizations, themselves, started to sponsor conferences. The first annual Omaha (Nebraska) Writers' Conference was set and sponsored by the Nebraska Writers' Guild; the Pacific Northwest Writers' Conference was held in Seattle, Washington, sponsored by the Pacific Northwest Writers' Association. By 1948, *Publisher's Weekly* could refer to editors and publishers "setting forth on the annual summer circuit of college, university and regional writers' conferences." By now a dozen programs were offered, and faculty, as well as conference themes and costs, were listed.

The first hints of specialization came in the early 1950s, as some writers' conferences began to see themselves unable or unwilling to offer all things to all writers. Conferences specializing in mystery writing developed, as did those in fiction writing and poetry. By some estimates there were more than one million Americans seeking to be writers. One writer, himself a Catholic, suggested there should be a Catholic-directed writers' conference to broaden the appeal of settled Catholic morality and instill it in the development of Catholic writers. More than one-sixth of all Americans are Catholic, this writer wrote in *Catholic World*, "but it is very uncertain that we have one-sixth of the good writers. You could count all the first-class Catholic novelists in this country on your fingers, and you might have some fingers left."

Along with the move towards specialization came variations on the "Bread Loaf Idea" that writers' conferences must run two weeks. Three- to five-day conferences sprung up, using an accelerated curriculum, and—surprise!—they were successful. So much so, in fact, that by 1955 short-form writers' conferences, as well as the two-week variety, were available in every section of the country, though they remained concentrated in the East and Midwest. Yet more than thirty conference opportunities were now possible.

And the momentum continued. By the mid-1960s, *Saturday Review* would list forty three conference choices across the country in its annual April roundup. By now the short-form and longform varieties were clearly accepted and categorized; there were the one- to four-day conferences and there were the one- to two-week conferences. Each had its value, though Gorham Munson set out two basic questions common for both: "Does [the conference] offer really good writers to lead the workshops? Does it provide a friendly, informal environment for the conferees?"

In effect, the writers'-conference idea had come full circle because these questions were the basis forty years earlier for the creation of Bread Loaf. Good writers to lead workshops... informal settings in which to learn and absorb. In a generation and a half the writers' conference had become a cultural standard and a solid pillar for writing success.

But changes in overall scope kept coming. By the early 1970s writers' conferences in Christian writing had multiplied, as the move towards specialization continued. In 1973, for example, *Decision Magazine*'s School of Christian Writing attracted 1900 inquiries, 400 applications for 200-250 places. Three Christian-writing programs were scheduled for California, and individual programs were set in Minnesota, Illinois, Oregon, Wisconsin and New York. No longer was religious writing a step-child in the creative-writing family. It was now included along with Bread Loaf and Iowa in any listing of "summertime writers' conference opportunities." Specialization, of course, didn't stop here. *Time Magazine* could report in 1977 there were about ninety writers' conferences now available during the summer, including "a Mystery Writers' Conference in Aptos, California, a New England

Conference in Children's literature at Northhampton, Massachu-setts. Beach-loving authors could even soak up inspiration at the Carribbean Writers' Workshop in the Virgin Islands."

And by 1980 specialization was even further developed. *The Writer* magazine, in an annual summary, could list 121 writers' conferences in thirty one states; among them were: "Writers' Con-ference in Children's Literature... Black Writer's Workshop... Cabrillo Suspense Writers' Conference... Christian Writers' Con-ference... Writing Workshop for People Over 57... Clarion Science Fiction Writers' Workshop... Annual Outdoor Writers' Association Conference..." The writers'-conference idea was now a cornucopia of possibilities, and no matter where the writer lived, a writers' conference that catered to his or her special interests was available and convenient.

In two generations writers' conferences had progressed from one tentative model in a remote section of Vermont to hardy, an-nual programs in many states, sometimes urbanized, sometimes—following the Bread Loaf lead—nested in a private aerie. As the 1980s and 1990s progressed, the conference numbers continued to proliferate (in 1987, for example, *The Writer* listed 140 summer conferences in forty two states; in 1993 there were 152 conferences listed in forty three states), yet one thing never varied. Those who came to the writers' conferences, who paid their money and sought confirmation of their talents, were no different from those who had come to the Rocky Mountain Conference in 1935: then, it had been "newspaper and advertising reporters, housewives, school teachers..."; almost fifty years later at a confer-ence in La Jolla, CA, according to *Publishers Weekly*, it was an "ophthalmologist, musician, investment banker, phototechnician, attorney, psychologist..." who would come.

As things go, the Writers' Conference has reached a comfort-able, secure place in what it takes to prod writing success. John Ciardi said it and most echo it: "*Every* writer I can think of was at one time a member of a group..."

The
Complete
Guide
to Writers'
Conferences
and
Workshops

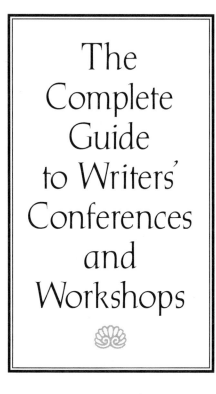

ALABAMA

SOUTHERN CHRISTIAN WRITERS' CONFERENCE

P.O. Box 1106
Northport, AL 35476
tel: (205) 333-8603

A weekend conference with workshops "geared to Christians or any other interested writers who want to write for Christian or secular magazines or books. All the speakers are Christians who come from varied denominations." Covered are fiction (including mystery and romance), nonfiction, essay, children's literature, song writing.

Director/Contact: Joanne Sloan, Coordinator

Location (s): Dwight Beeson Auditorium, Samford University, Birmingham, AL

Dates: June, 1996

Commenced: 1994

Recent faculty/lecturers: Mike Yorkey, Patricia Sprinkle, Marion Bond West, Kay Cornelius, Deborah Brunt, Margaret Searcy, Harold Jackson

Agents/editors attend: yes; *Available for conferencing:* on an informal basis

Enrollment: 100-200; *Enrollment limit:* 250

Ancillary activities: author book sales, door-prize drawing

WRITING AND ILLUSTRATING FOR KIDS

Annual Spring Conference
Annual Fall Conference
Alabama-Georgia Region Society of
Children's Book Writers and Illustrators
1616 Kestwick Drive
Birmingham, AL 35226
tel: (205) 979-0270

One- and two-day conferences and workshops geared specifically to the production and support of quality children's literature. The spring conference contains no workshops, but there are fourteen workshops in the fall conference for entry-level and professional writers. Both conferences provide numerous talks on craft from early picture books through young adult novels.

Director/Contact: Joan Broerman, Regional Advisor

Location(s): Quality Inn Beachside, Gulfshores, AL (spring); Birmingham Botanical Gardens, Birmingham, AL (fall)

Dates: February 23, 24, 1996; October 19, 1996

Commenced: 1993 (spring); 1992 (fall)

Recent faculty/lecturers: spring—Eha Wilson, Laurie Myers, Robert Burch, Evelyn Coleman; fall—Cheryl Zach, Larry Dane Brimner, Faye Gibbons, Betsey Duffey

Manuscripts: not required, but manuscript critiques and portfolio reviews are available. *Note:* "any manuscript submissions must contain an SASE, or they will be placed on the bottom of the pile"; *Individual manuscript conferencing:* yes; *Editing assistance:* yes; *Marketing guidance:* yes

Agents and editors attend: yes; *Available for conferencing:* yes

Enrollment: 75; *Enrollment limit:* up to 300; workshops may be limited, depending upon speakers' preferences

Writing Today

Office of Special Events
Birmingham Southern College
900 Arkadelphia Road, Box A-3
Birmingham, AL 35254
tel: (205) 226-4921
fax: (205) 226-4931

Two-day conference sponsored by and held on the campus of Birmingham-Southern College, Birmingham, AL, with workshops on fiction, nonfiction, poetry, play writing and film.

Director/Contact: Martha Andrews, Director

Location (s): Birmingham-Southern College, Birmingham, AL

Dates: March, 1996

Commenced: 1981

Recent faculty/lecturers: Gwendolyn Brooks, Willie Morris, Bharati Mukherjee, Barbara Parks, Howell Raines

Editing assistance: yes; *Marketing guidance:* yes

Agents/editors attend: yes; *Available for conferencing:* yes

Enrollment: 570; *Enrollment limit:* 600

Scholarships: available to area high school students only

Ancillary activities: readings by well-known authors; annual Hackney Literary Awards Contest, winners receiving prizes in novel, short story and poetry categories and announced at conference

ARIZONA

AMERICAN CHRISTIAN WRITERS' CONFERENCES
Box 5168
Phoenix, AZ 85010
tel: (800) 21-WRITE

Three-day conferences and workshops on fiction, nonfiction, poetry, play writing, film, television, video in Phoenix and at numerous other sites across the country throughout the year, including a "beginning writers' day," an "advanced writers' day," a "songwriters' day."

Director/Contact: Reg A. Forder, Director

Location(s): Phoenix Airport Days Inn

Dates: November, 1996

Commenced: 1981

Recent faculty/lecturers: Donna Partow, Susan Titus Osborn, Tom McLain, Mona Hodgson

Individual manuscript conferencing: yes; *Editing assistance:* yes; *Marketing guidance:* yes

Agents/editors attend: yes; *Available for conferencing:* yes

Enrollment: 200

Scholarships: yes; call or write for details

Ancillary activities: books and tapes by mail order, monthly writers' magazine, Caribbean writers' cruise, 36-lesson writing course via correspondence school

DESERT DREAMS WRITERS' CONFERENCE
1482 E. Butler Circle
Chandler, AZ 85225-5788
tel: (602) 917-8041
fax: (602) 917-8066

A three-day "comprehensive writers' conference encompassing all aspects of the Romance genre. Twenty-four educational workshops, editor/agent brunch," sponsored by the Phoenix Desert Rose Chapter of the Romance Writers of America.

Director/Contact: Patricia R. Jennings, Conference Coordinator

Location(s): Tempe Radisson Mission Palms Hotel, Tempe, AZ

Dates: mid-September, 1996

Commenced: 1984

Recent faculty/lecturers: Parris Afton Bonds, Connie Flynn Alexander, Robin Lee Hatcher, Jane Kidder, Heather Graham, Meryl Sawyer

Marketing guidance: yes

Agents/editors attend: yes; *Available for conferencing:* yes

Enrollment: 300

Ancillary activities: autograph luncheon

GILA WRITERS' CONFERENCE
11012 E. Crescent Avenue
Apache Junction, AZ 85220
tel: (602) 986-1399

This two- or three-day conference connected to Western New Mexico University has "sessions on fiction, nonfiction, poetry, screenwriting, writing for children, publishing."

Director/Contact: Meg Files, Robert M. Powers, Co-Directors

Location(s): Silver City, New Mexico

Dates: August, 1996

Commenced: 1994

Recent faculty/lecturers: Joanne Greenberg, Allen Woodman, Frank Gaspar, Sharman Russell

Individual manuscript conferencing: yes; *Editing assistance:* yes; *Marketing guidance:* yes

Agents/editors attend: yes; *Available for conferencing:* yes

Enrollment: 60—no enrollment limit

Ancillary activities: readings, panels, films, writing exercises

PIMA WRITERS' WORKSHOP
Pima College
2202 W. Anklam Road
Tucson, AZ 85709
tel: (602) 884-6974
fax: (602) 884-6975

A three-day conference that offers workshops on "fiction, nonfiction, poetry, screenwriting, writing for children, publishing."

Director/Contact: Meg Files, Director

Location(s): campus of Pima College, Tucson, AZ

Dates: May, 1996

Commenced: 1987

Recent faculty/lecturers: Larry McMurtry, Brian Garfield, Barbara Kingsolver, Nancy Mairs, Ron Carlson, Linda McCarriston

Individual manuscript conferencing: yes; *Marketing guidance:* yes

Agents/editors attend: yes; *Available for conferencing:* yes

Enrollment: 200—no enrollment limit

Ancillary activities: readings, panels, writing exercises

READER'S DIGEST WRITERS' WORKSHOP

NAU Box 5638
Northern Arizona University
Flagstaff, AZ 86011
tel: (602) 523-3559
fax: (602) 523-1711

"This workshop focuses upon bringing together leading nonfiction magazine editors with free-lance writers who wish to enter the major magazine marketplace. Emphasis is upon practical 'how to do' counseling and teaching."

Director/Contact: Ray Newton, Administrator/Professor

Location(s): Las Vegas, NV

Dates: May, 1996

Commenced: 1974

Recent faculty/lecturers: major magazine editors

Agents/editors attend: yes; *Available for conferencing:* yes

Enrollment: 200; *Enrollment limit:* 225

Ancillary activities: individual sessions with editors/reputable writers

ARKANSAS

ARKANSAS WRITERS' CONFERENCE

1115 Gillette Drive
Little Rock, AR 72227
tel: (501) 225-0166

A weekend conference featuring speakers and panels on fiction, nonfiction, poetry, film, television and "on various subjects related to writing."

Director/Contact: Clovita Rice, Director

Location(s): Holiday Inn West, Little Rock, AR

Dates: first weekend in June, 1996

Commenced: 1944

Recent faculty/lecturers: Sharon Linnea, Peter Miller, Gene Lyons

Individual manuscript conferencing: yes; *Marketing guidance:* yes

Agents/editors attend: yes

Enrollment: 225

Ancillary activities: readings, banquet, book display and sale, 46 separate writing contests in fiction, nonfiction, poetry, humor, children's literature

OSARK CREATIVE WRITERS' CONFERENCE
511 Perry Road
Springdale, AR 72764
tel: (501) 251-7246

Three-day conference with workshops in "fiction, articles, poetry, song writing," sponsored by a nonprofit organization that encourages creative writing.

Director/Contact: Dusty Richards, President

Location(s): Inn of the Osarks Conference Center, Eureka Springs, AR

Dates: Oct. 11-13, 1996

Commenced: 1969

Recent faculty/lecturers: John Burns Cooke, Dale Walker, Mona Sizer, Lisa Wingate, Velda Brotherton, Frederic Bean, W.C. Jameson

Agents/editors attend: yes; *Available for conferencing:* yes

Enrollment: 200 plus

Ancillary activities: contests in all writing categories

WHITE RIVER WRITERS' WORKSHOP

P.O. Box 2317
Lyon College
Batesville, AR 72503-2317
tel: (501) 793-1766
fax: (501) 698-4622

A one-week poetry program which "offers serious poets the opportunity to work on new and in-progress poems or translations in small, concentrated workshops... Mornings are spent in workshop, in individual conference, in writing or translating poems." Afternoons are devoted to lectures, panels and participant readings with evenings given over to faculty and fellow readings.

Director/Contact: Andrea Hollander Budy, Director

Location (s): campus of Lyon College, Batesville, AR

Dates: mid-late June, 1996

Commenced: 1995

Recent faculty/lecturers: Dana Gioia, Linda Gregg, Lola Haskins, Ted Kooser, Susan Ludvigson, Lee Potts

Manuscript: required; *Individual manuscript conferencing:* yes; *Editing assistance:* yes; *Marketing guidance:* yes

Agents/editors attend: yes; *Available for conferencing:* yes

Enrollment: 50; *Enrollment limit:* 50

Scholarships: yes

Ancillary activities: readings, receptions, socials

CALIFORNIA

❀

AMERICAN CHRISTIAN WRITERS' CONFERENCE
(held in San Diego, CA in March, 1996—
see Arizona for details)

BOOK PASSAGE
Mystery Writers' Conference
Travel Writers' Conference
51 Tamal Vista
Corte Madera, CA 94925
tel: (415) 927-0960 • *fax:* (415) 924-3838

MYSTERY WRITING: four-day conference covering the initial idea to the shelf in the bookstore, including witnessing and investigating a simulated crime scene, writing the story, developing plot, character, suspense, setting, understanding the mystery market and workshops with crime specialists.

TRAVEL WRITING: four-day conference covering all forms of travel writing, from guidebooks to newspaper articles, including writing workshops, photography workshops, travel trends in newspapers, magazines and book publishing.

Director/Contact: Kathryn Barcos (Mystery), Marguerite Castanera (Travel)

Location(s): Book Passage (bookstore) and The Corte Madera Inn

Dates: mid-July (Mystery), late August (Travel), 1996

Commenced: 1994 (Mystery), 1991 (Travel)

Recent faculty/lecturers: Mystery: Margaret Maron, Linda Grant, Robert Crais, John Lescroart; Travel: Jan Morris, Arthur Frommer, Barbara Peck, Pico Iyer

Individual manuscript conferencing: yes, for both; *Marketing guidance:* yes, for both

Agents/editors attend: yes, for both; *Available for conferencing:* yes, for both

Enrollment: 100 in each; *Enrollment limit:* 100 in each

Ancillary activities:

– MYSTERY: an acted murder scene at the opening banquet; students are asked to write how it ends, how it started. These are read at the closing ceremony

– TRAVEL: a writing/essay contest based on a chosen travel-writing theme. Winner is given free round trip airfare to Italy and London,courtesy of British Airways, co-sponsor oftravel portion of conference

CHRISTIAN COMMUNICATORS CONFERENCE
3133 Puente Street
Fullerton, CA 92635
tel: (714) 990-1532
fax: (714) 990-0310

A four-day conference covering "five morning continuing classes and thirty afternoon workshops in fiction, nonfiction books, article writing, writing for children, poetry, screenplays, beginning writing, marketing and editing."

Director/Contact: Susan Titus Osborn, Co-director

Location(s): The Masters College, Santa Clarita, CA

Dates: July 18-21, 1996

Commenced: 1994 (previously held at Biola University)

Recent faculty/lecturers: John MacArthur, Harold Ivan Smith, Liz Curtis Higgs, Wightman Weese

Individual manuscript conferencing: yes; *Editing assistance:* yes; *Marketing guidance:* yes

Agents/editors attend: yes; *Available for conferencing:* yes

Enrollment: 150; Enrollment limit: 200

Ancillary activities: manuscript critique service; college credit
(1 unit) or 1 continuing education unit (CEU)

FOOTHILL WRITERS' CONFERENCE

Foothill College
12345 El Monte Road
Los Altos Hills, CA 94022-4599
tel: (415) 949-7316

One-week conference with "poetry, fiction and nonfiction
workshops; lectures and panels on special topics; one-on-one poetry
sessions; poetry readings daily."

Director/Contact: Dick Maxwell, Professor of English and Creative
Writing

Location(s): Foothill College

Dates: June 27-July 2, 1996

Commenced: 1974

Recent faculty/lecturers: Garret Hongo, Jane Hirshfield, Al Young,
Alan Cheuse

Manuscripts: yes; *Individual manuscript conferencing:* yes; *Editing
assistance:* yes; *Marketing guidance:* yes

Enrollment: 200

MENDOCINO COAST WRITERS' CONFERENCE
College of the Redwoods
1211 Del Mar Drive
Fort Bragg, CA 95437
tel: (707) 961-1001

A weekend conference bringing together "writers, editors, agents and publishers who will give presentations to the general assembly as well as conduct workshops and hold private consultations" in fiction (including historical, mystery and science fiction), children's literature, nonfiction, poetry, play writing.

Director/Contact: Marlis Manley Broadhead, Director

Location(s): College of the Redwoods, Fort Bragg, CA

Dates: 1st weekend in June, 1996

Commenced: 1990

Recent faculty/lecturers: Shiela Bender, Dorothy Bryant, Elizabeth Cox, Jerry Juhl, Elizabeth Tallent, Linda Grant

Individual manuscript conferencing: yes; *Editing assistance:* yes; *Marketing guidance:* yes

Agents/editors attend: yes; *Available for conferencing:* yes

Enrollment: 130

Scholarships: yes—a limited number

Ancillary activities: River Rhyme Poetry Contest; books and hospitality room, party

MIND MOVES
P.O. Box 2201
La Jolla, CA 92038-2201
tel: (619) 459-8897

One- and two-day weekend "writeshops" featuring creativity in writing and expression with poetry, essays, memoirs and short fiction. Workshops call upon "other" arts such as music, painting, mythology to stimulate the writing process.

Director/Contact: Penny Wilkes, Director

Location(s): San Diego, CA

Dates: periodic weekends, January-June, 1996

Commenced: 1989

Recent faculty/lecturers: local writers, artists, musicians

Manuscripts: required; *Individual manuscript conferencing:* yes; *Editing guidance:* yes

Enrollment: 8 in small sessions—no enrollment limit

MOUNT HERMON CHRISTIAN WRITERS' CONFERENCE
P.O. Box 413
Mount Hermon, CA 95041
tel: (408) 335-4466 • *fax:* (408) 335-9218

Five-day conference/workshop covering "all aspects of writing for the Christian market, including general beginners basics, plus advanced track."

Director/Contact: David R. Talbott, Director of Specialized Programs

Location(s): Mount Hermon Christian Conference Center, Mount Herman, CA

Dates: March 29-April 2, 1996

Commenced: 1969

Recent faculty/lecturers: Charles Swindell, Calvin Miller, Jerry Jenkins, Ted Engstrom

Editing assistance: yes; *Marketing guidance:* yes

Agents/editors attend: yes; *Available for conferencing:* yes

Enrollment: 200; *Enrollment limit:* 400

Scholarships: available; a campership application form must be requested and submitted

PAUL GILLETTE'S WRITERS' WORKSHOP
3284 Barham Blvd (#20)
Los Angeles, CA 90068-2454
tel: (213) 876-7590
fax: (213) 876-4090

A regular, weekly/monthly program dealing with fiction, nonfiction, play writing, film, television and video.

Director/Contact: Paul Gillette

Location (s): Los Angeles, CA

Dates: first 4 Wednesdays of each month

Commenced: 1976

Recent faculty/lecturers: Paul Gillette

Individual manuscript conferencing: yes; *Editing assistance:* yes; *Marketing guidance:* yes

Agents/editors attend: yes; *Available for conferencing:* yes

Enrollment: 25; *Enrollment limit:* 25

Ancillary activities: assistance in meeting producers (television, film, play), managers, editors, agents

SAN DIEGO CHRISTIAN WRITERS' GUILD SEMINAR
Box 1171
El Cajon, CA 92022
tel: (619) 748-0565

One-day program dealing with fiction, nonfiction, poetry, play writing, song writing.

Director/Contact: Dr. Sherwood E. Wirt, Convener

Location(s): Horizon Christian Fellowship, 5331 Mt. Alifan Drive, San Diego, CA 92111

Dates: September, 1996

Commenced: 1977

Recent faculty/lecturers: Jerry Jenkins, Ernest E. Owen, Leslie Stobbe, Carole Gift Page, Carole Carlson

Individual manuscript conferencing: yes; *Marketing guidance:* yes

Agents/editors attend: yes; *Available for conferencing:* yes

Enrollment: 150

Scholarships: yes, for local county residents only

Ancillary activities: Spring-Awards Night Banquet, naming of writer of the year

SAN DIEGO STATE UNIVERSITY WRITERS' CONFERENCE
SDSU College of Extended Studies
5250 Campanile Drive
San Diego, CA 92182-1920
tel: (619) 594-5152

Two-day conference on "screenwriting, fiction, nonfiction, children's writing," and a "research emporium" which "has been created to help writers research areas common to both fiction and nonfiction."

Director/Contact: Diane Dunaway, Coordinator

Location(s): Montezuma Hall, Aztec Center, SDSU

Dates: January 20-21, 1996

Commenced: 1984

Recent faculty/lecturers: Carol Roper, Erin Grady, Laura Taylor, Deborah Nourse Lattimore, Diane Gage, Jonathan Kramer, PhD

Individual manuscript conferencing: yes; *Editing assistance:* yes; *Marketing guidance:* yes

Agents/editors attend: yes; *Available for conferencing:* yes

Enrollment: 400; *Enrollment limit:* 400

Ancillary acitivities: "read and critique" of participants' submissions; wine and cheese reception following final session

SANTA BARBARA WRITERS' CONFERENCE
P.O. Box 304
Carpenteria, CA 93014
tel: (805) 684-2250
fax: (805) 684-2250

A one-week conference presenting 25 workshops in fiction, nonfiction, poetry, screenwriting, play writing, as well as specific genres within these categories, including mystery, horror, humor, biography, travel. Credits are available from University of California, Santa Barbara.

Director/Contact: Mary or Barnaby Conrad

Location(s): Miramar Hotel, Santa Barbara, CA

Dates: June 21-28, 1996

Commenced: 1973

Recent faculty/lecturers: Ray Bradbury, Charles Schultz, Harriet Doerr, Robert Fulghum, Jules Feiffer, James Michener

Individual manuscript conferencing: yes; *Editing assistance:* yes; *Marketing guidance:* yes

Agents/editors attend: yes; *Available for conferencing:* yes

Enrollment: 350; *Enrollment limit:* 350

Scholarships: available; apply directly to Santa Barbara Writers' Conference

Ancillary activities: readings, publications, contests

SANTA MONICA COLLEGE WRITERS' CONFERENCE
English Department
Santa Monica College
1900 Pico Blvd.
Santa Monica, CA 90405
tel: (310) 452-9242

A five-day conference that "brings together four nationally-acclaimed authors for a week's intensive discussion and writing of poetry. Each day will include a reading and craft lecture by one of the four leaders. The readings and lecture will be followed by process workshops which will focus on challenging new writing assignments."

Director/Contact: Cathleen Long, Director

Location(s): Santa Monica College, Santa Monica, CA

Dates: mid-June, 1996

Commenced: 1987

Recent faculty/lecturers: Charles Baxter, Ann Beattie, Garret Hongo. Philp Levine, Sandra McPherson, Alicia Ostriker, Grace Paley, Walter Pavlich, Mona Simpson

Manuscripts: required; *Individual manuscript conferencing:* yes; *Editing assistance:* yes; *Marketing guidance:* yes

Enrollment: 70 including full-time participants and auditors; *Enrollment limit:* 48 full-time participants

Ancillary activities: morning readings and panel discussions

MEET ... CATHY LONG

DIRECTOR, SANTA MONICA COLLEGE (CA) WRITERS' CONFERENCE

SOME WRITERS'-CONFERENCE DIRECTORS have a win-win situation! Working and living in southern California, a few moments from the Pacific, it's not hard to conjure an idyll of physical comfort and sublime creative fulfillment. Allowing others to share the dream—even temporarily—is to savor high pleasure amidst the crunching demands of writing. But Cathy Long, Director of the Santa Monica College Writers' Conference, prefers to concentrate on the writing and leave emphasis on the benign climate to others. "I want our focus to be literary," she says. "If I were to advise prospective students preparing to come to our conference, I'd tell them to write, write, write!"

Long, a graduate of the University of Illinois with a graduate degree from the University of Chicago, was one of the founders of the Santa Monica College Writers' Conference. Before that she attended conferences in Napa (California) and Port Townsend (Washington), and "I was really excited about the whole idea of writers' conferences." But these sites were hundreds of miles away, and as a member of the English Department faculty at Santa Monica College, she was offered an opportunity to develop a home-grown conference. "I wanted to see something closer to Los Angeles," she says, and with colleague Jim Krusoe she was able to get things started.

For the first six years the focus was on fiction; Long and Krusoe offered a number of renowned fiction writers, including Mona Simpson, Ann Beattie, Ron Carlson, Joy Williams, Helena

Viramontes, Elizabeth Tallent, Denis Johnson, Grace Paley and Charles Baxter. But Krusoe was also founder of the *Santa Monica Review*, and as his responsibilities grew there, Cathy Long took over direction of the writers' conference. By 1993 Long was directing the conference with other faculty members, and now the writers' conference shifted gears. The emphasis became poetry, and Long could offer poets such as David St. John, Sandra McPherson, Walter Pavlich, Alberto Rios, Alicia Ostriker, Philip Levine, Pattiann Rogers and Diane Wakoski. The move to poetry was comfortable for Long because she is, herself, a published poet, reading her work throughout California and appearing in literary magazines such as *Poetry/LA, Verve, California Quarterly*, among others. Her work has been anthologized, and she was, formerly, an editor of *The Sculpture Garden Review*.

The Santa Monica College Writers' Conference accepts forty-eight students each year. "The program lasts for one week," Long says. "We have four faculty leaders, and then there are morning readings [open to the community for a modest fee], followed by workshops, lunch, afternoon workshops, and on Fridays, there's a big picnic." She breaks the students into four groups to complement the four faculty leaders, and the groups stay together during the week. That means there are no more than twelve in any group. "What's special about our conference is that the groups rotate from day to day so that each  person gets to work with all the faculty members." She understands that with many writers' conferences, the student chooses one faculty member and that's with whom he or she works throughout the conference. "My personal experience is that it's better if you can work with all the faculty."

Cathy Long is pleased with how the Santa Monica College Writers' Conference has developed. "I think we have an extraordinarily successful writers' conference," she says, "it's been so enriching for me, so satisfying. It's really been more successful than I could have ever dreamed it would have been."

And the benign climate? That certainly can't hurt.

SQUAW VALLEY COMMUNITY OF WRITERS
P.O. Box 2352
Olympic Valley, CA 96146
tel: (916) 583-5200 (summer) • (415) 389-5931 (winter)
fax: (916) 583-5200 (summer)—call first
(415) 389-5931 (winter)—call first

FICTION PROGRAM
"Offers a week of formal and informal workshops, seminars, panel discussions, staff readings and craft lectures. Morning formal workshops are led by the writer-teachers, editors and agents of the staff." nonfiction manuscripts are included in the fiction workshops.

Director/Contact: Brett Hall Jones, Executive Director; Oakley Hall, General Director

Location (s): Squaw Valley, CA

Dates: August 3-10, 1996

Commenced: 1970

Recent faculty/lecturers: Ron Hansen, Robert Stone, Mary Morris, Anne Lamott, Richard Ford, Louis Owens, Sandra Scofield

Manuscripts: required; *Individual manuscript conferencing:* yes; *Editing assistance:* yes; *Marketing guidance:* yes

Agents/editors attend: yes; *Available for conferencing:* yes

Enrollment: 125; *Enrollment limit:* 125

Scholarships: yes

Ancillary activities: readings, craft lectures, agent and editor panels, bi-annual newsletter

POETRY PROGRAM

A one-week program with workshops that encourage participants to "try to break through old habits and write something daring and difficult... Groups meet each morning for about two hours to discuss the work of the previous twenty-four hours, and meet each afternoon for a session on craft. At other times of the day participants are writing."

Director/Contact: Brett Hall Jones, Executive Director; Oakley Hall, General Director

Location(s): Squaw Valley, CA

Dates: late July, 1996

Commenced: 1970

Recent faculty/lecturers: Sharon Olds, Galway Kinnell, Lucille Clifton, Luci Tapahonso, Robert Hass, Brenda Hillman

Manuscript: required; *Individual manuscript conferencing:* yes

Enrollment: 52; *Enrollment limit:* 52

Scholarships: yes

Ancillary activities: readings, craft lectures, publication of *The Squaw Review*, an anthology of poems written during the week

SCREENWRITING PROGRAM

"An intensive week of workshops with emphasis on the grammar of screenwriting, narrative point-of-view, and especially on finding the 'story'. The program is designed for screenwriters and fiction writers and playwrights who wish to translate their work into the film medium."

Director/Contact: Diana Fuller, Screenwriting Director; Brett Hall Jones, Executive Director; Oakley Hall, General Director

Location(s): Squaw Valley, CA

Dates: August 2-10, 1996

Commenced: 1978

Recent faculty/lecturers: Tom Rickman, Gill Dennis, Frank Pierson, Antonio Tibaldi, Barbara Schultz, Ruth Shapiro, Judith Rascoe

Manuscript: required; *Individual manuscript conferencing:* yes; *Editing assistance:* yes; *Marketing guidance:* yes

Agents/editors attend: yes; *Available for conferencing:* yes

Enrollment: 18-20; *Enrollment limit:* yes

Scholarships: yes

Ancillary activities: participation in the afternoon and evening fiction events is encouraged

WRITERS' CONFERENCE IN CHILDREN'S LITERATURE
22736 Van Owen Street, Suite 106
West Hills, CA 91307
tel: (818) 888-8760

Four-day conference sponsored by the Society of Children's Book Writers and Illustrators and UCLA Extension on all forms of children's book writing and illustrating, including magazine writing, picture-book writing, novel writing, nonfiction writing.

Director/Contact: Lin Oliver

Location(s): Doubletree Hotel, Marina del Rey, CA

Dates: mid-August, 1996

Commenced: 1972

Recent faculty/lecturers: Paula Danziger, Jim Murphy, Dan Stern, Mary Downing Hahn, Ann M. Martin, Stephan Mooser

Individual manuscript conferencing: yes; *Editing assistance:* yes; *Marketing guidance:* yes

Agents/editors attend: yes; *Available for conferencing:* yes

Enrollment: 400; *Enrollment limit:* 450

Ancillary activities: small critique groups at the end of each day

WRITERS' CONNECTION

P.O. Box 24770
San Jose, CA 95154-4770
tel: (408) 445-3600
fax: (408) 445-3609

An organization that puts on several weekend conferences during the year. Topics have included "Selling to Hollywood," "Writing Children's Picture Books," "Writing For Interactive Multimedia," and the workshops include writing, production and selling to specific markets.

Director/Contact: Writers Connection

Location(s): Red Lion Hotel, Glendale, CA

Dates: August, 1996 (for "Selling to Hollywood"), others periodic throughout the year

Recent faculty/lecturers: Jeff Arch (scriptwriter, "Sleepless in Seattle"), Bruce Singer, Madeline DiMaggio, John Vorhaus, Rick Reichman

Individual manuscript conferencing: yes; *Marketing guidance:* yes

Agents/editors/producers attend: yes; *Available for conferencing:* yes

Enrollment: 200; *Enrollment limit:* 300

WRITER'S DAY

Southern California Society of
Children's Book Writers and Illustrators
11943 Montana
Los Angeles, CA 90049
tel: (310) 820-5601
fax: (310) 826-2860

One-day conference on "writing and marketing in the fields of children's literature. Features published authors, agents, editors."

Director/Contact: S. Tessler, J. Enderle, Regional Advisors

Dates: Spring, 1996

Commenced: 1989

Recent faculty/lecturers: Patricia Polacco, Jeanette Larson, Sheri Cooper Sinykin, Sandra Arnold

Marketing guidance: yes

Agents/editors attend: yes; *Available for conferencing:* yes, on an informal basis

Enrollment: 125; *Enrollment limit:* 150

Ancillary activities: writing contest for attendees

WRITER'S FORUM

Pasadena City College, Community Education Dept.
1570 East Colorado Blvd
Pasadena, CA 91006
tel: (818) 585-7609
fax: (818) 585-7910

One-day conference put on by Pasadena City College which includes all phases of writing: fiction, nonfiction, poetry, script writing, children's writing. There are nine speakers plus a panel of editors, agents, authors.

Director/Contact: Meredith Brucker, Coordinator

Location(s): campus of Pasadena City College, Pasadena, CA

Dates: March, 1996

Commenced: 1954

Recent faculty/lecturers: Eve Bunting (childrens' books), Kenneth Atchity (motivation), John M. Wilson (nonfiction), Neill Hicks (screenplays)

Manuscripts: not required; *Marketing guidance:* yes

Agents/editors attend: yes, but not available for conferencing

Enrollment: 200—no enrollment limit

Scholarships: discounts available at time of registration for high school and Pasadena City College students

Ancillary activities: a book stall is operated by a local bookstore

COLORADO

COLORADO CHRISTIAN WRITERS' CONFERENCE

67 Seminole Court
Lyons, CO 80540
tel: (303) 823-5718

Three-day conference with symposia and fifty six workshops (including a track for advanced authors) on "all forms of writing [fiction, nonfiction, poetry, children's literature, song writing] and publishing relevant to Christians who write and desire to transform society with truth and beauty through literature."

Director/Contact: Debbie Barker, Director

Location(s): Boulder, CO area

Dates: March 7-9, 1996

Commenced: 1984

Recent faculty/lecturers: Dr. Gene Edward Veith, Ronald Klug, Marva Dawn, Gretchen Passantino, Ethel Herr, Bill Myers, James Riordan

Individual manuscript conferencing: yes; *Editing assistance:* yes; *Marketing guidance:* yes

Agents editors attend: yes; *Available for conferencing:* yes

Enrollment: 250

Scholarships: available; apply to the director

Ancillary activities: critique sessions, autograph booths, a pizza party, book consignment table

COLORADO GOLD CONFERENCE
Rocky Mountain Fiction Writers
P.O. Box 260244
Denver, CO 80226-0244
tel: (303) 252-7520

Three-day conference sponsored by Rocky Mountain Fiction Writers and "designed for writers of novel-length commercial fiction, [allowing] attendees to meet editors and agents from both small and major houses, to workshop material with published authors and to hear expert speakers on topics of interest."

Director/Contact: Sharon Mignerey, Co-Chair

Location(s): Sheraton Hotel, Lakewood, CO

Dates: September 6-8, 1996

Commenced: 1983

Recent faculty/lecturers: Dorothy Cannell, James Frye, Jack Bickham, Clive Cussler, Joan Hess, Sandra Canfield

Individual manuscript conferencing: yes; *Editing assistance:* yes; *Marketing guidance:* yes

Agents/editors attend: yes; *Available for conferencing:* yes

Enrollment: 250; *Enrollment limit:* 300

Ancillary activities: annual contest for unpublished writers, monthly newsletter for RMFW members

Colorado Mountain Writers' Workshop
3000 County Road 114
Glenwood Springs, CO 81601
tel: (303) 945-7481
fax: (303) 945-1227

A five-day conference with workshops that focus on fiction and poetry. There are lectures, panels, films and special events.

Director/Contact: Doug Evans, Director

Location(s): campus of Colorado Mountain College, Glenwood, CO

Dates: July 22-26, 1996

Commenced: 1978

Recent faculty/lecturers: Carolyn Forche, Joanne Greenberg, Lyn Lifshin, James Dickey, Harlan Ellison, Edward Bryant

Individual manuscript conferencing: yes; *Editing assistance:* yes; *Marketing guidance:* yes

Enrollment: 50; *Enrollment limit:* 50

Ancillary activities: readings, parties

Ladan Reserve Annual Women's Conference
Box 881239
Steamboat Plaza, CO 80488
tel: (303) 723-4953
fax: (303) 723-4918

First annual writers' conference on "women's literature today. A conference/symposium, not a workshop. Participants by invitation only. Symposiums are open to the public and students."

Director/Contact: Jeffrey Hayden, President

Location(s): rural Colorado

Dates: July 1-6, 1996

Commenced: 1996

Agents/editors attend: yes; *Available for conferencing:* yes

Enrollment: 50

Ancillary activities: readings, symposiums, guest lecture

NATIONAL WRITERS ASSOCIATION
SUMMER CONFERENCE
1450 S. Havana
Suite 424
Aurora, CO 80012
tel: (303) 751-7844
fax: (303) 751-8593

Twelve sessions (each repeated once) over three days on various phases of writing, including fiction, nonfiction, poetry, with panels of editors and agents and one-on-one consultations.

Director/Contact: Sandy Whelchel, Executive Director

Location(s): Denver, CO area

Dates: June 15-17, 1996

Commenced: originally held during the 1970s, revived 1993

Recent faculty/lecturers: Ann Rule, Julie Castiglia, Gordon Burgett, John Tigges, Janet Gluckman

Individual manuscript conferencing: yes; *Marketing guidance:* yes

Agents/editors attend: yes; *Available for conferencing:* yes

Enrollment: 200—no enrollment limit

Scholarships: undecided; applicants should call and check

Ancillary activities: book signings, awards for contest winners, bookstore offering writers' books

Steamboat Springs Writer's Day
P.O. Box 774284
Steamboat Springs, CO 80477
tel: (303) 879- 9008

One-day conference sponsored by the Steamboat Springs Art Council with a program that varies from year to year in fiction, nonfiction, poetry, play writing.

Director/Contact: Harriet Freiberger, Director

Location (s): Steamboat Springs, CO

Dates: July 20, 1996

Commenced: 1981

Recent faculty/lecturers: Donald Rovell, Rex Burns, Robert Pugel

Marketing guidance: yes

Agents/editors attend: sometimes—but not available for conferencing

Enrollment: 25; *Enrollment limit:* 25

CONNECTICUT

WESLYAN WRITERS' CONFERENCE

Weslyan University
Middletown, CT 06459
tel: (203)685-3604
fax: (203) 347-3996

A one-week conference with "seminars, workshops and lectures in the novel, short story, fiction techniques, poetry, fiction-and-film, literary journalism, memoir. Advice from editors and publishers."

Director/Contact: Anne Greene, Director

Location(s): campus of Weslyan University, Middletown, CT

Dates: last week, June, 1996

Commenced: 1956

Recent faculty/lecturers: Joyce Carol Oates, Robert Olen Butler, Robert Stone, Amy Bloom, Donald Justice, Henry Taylor, Dana Gioia, James Gleick, David Halberstam, David McCullough, William Zinsser, Jane Smiley

Manuscript: optional; *Individual manuscript conferencing:* yes; *Editing assistance:* yes; *Marketing guidance:* yes

Agents/editors attend: yes; *Available for conferencing:* "possibly"

Enrollment: 100

Scholarships: yes, including the Davidoff Scholarships for Journalists; teaching fellowships are also available

Ancillary activities: readings by faculty and students

FLORIDA

AMERICAN CHRISTIAN WRITERS' CONFERENCE
(held in Miami, FL, October, 1996—see Arizona for details)

CHRISTIAN WRITERS' INSTITUTE
177 E. Crystal Lake Avenue
Lake Mary, FL 32746
tel: (407) 324-5465
fax: (407) 324-0209

"A variety of subjects are offered for magazine, book writing, script writing and poetry."

Director/Contact: Dottie McBroom, Director

Location(s): Orlando, FL

Dates: Feb 22-25, 1996

Commenced: 1945

Recent faculty/lecturers: Elizabeth Sherrill, Leonard and Sandra LeSourd, Brock and Bodie Thoene, Janet Thoma, David Hazard

Manuscript required: yes, for advanced sessions; *Editing assistance:* yes; *Marketing guidance:* yes

Editors attend: yes; *Available for conferencing:* yes

Enrollment: 175—no limit

Ancillary actitivies: contests, tutorials, advanced track, youth track, Spanish track

FLORIDA CHRISTIAN WRITERS' CONFERENCE

2600 South Park Avenue
Titusville, FL 32780
tel: (407) 269-6702
fax: (407) 383-1741

Four day conference on fiction, nonfiction, children's literature, verse-writing that "offers workshops for every skill level—beginner through advanced. Extended learning labs; forty eight individual workshops; an advanced writers track."

Director/Contact: Billie Wilson, Director

Location(s): Park Avenue Baptist Church and Retreat Center

Dates: January 25-29, 1996

Commenced: 1987

Recent faculty/lecturers: Dr. Calvin Miller, Peter Lord, Donna Fletcher Crow, Lissa Halls Johnson, Stan Baldwin, Lin Johnson

Manuscripts: not required but encouraged; *Individual manuscript conferencing:* yes; *Editing assistance:* yes; *Marketing guidance:* yes

Agents/editors attend: yes; *Available for conferencing:* yes

Enrollment: no limit

Scholarships: discounts available for alumni

Ancillary activities: there is a conference bookstore, and cassettes of all general sessions and workshops will be available. Fellowship and refreshments each evening

FLORIDA FIRST COAST WRITERS' CONFERENCE
Kent Campus, FCCJ
Box 109
3939 Roosevelt Blvd
Jacksonville, FL 32205

Two-day series of workshops on fiction, nonfiction, poetry, children's literature, humor "for aspiring novelists, poets, freelancers, as participants meet with professional writers, editors and agents."

Director/Contact: Howard Denson, Director

Location(s): campus of Florida Community College at Jacksonville

Dates: late March, early April, 1996

Commenced: 1986

Recent faculty/lecturers: Donald Justice, Elisabeth Graves, Gwendolyn Brooks, Harry Crews, Peter Taylor

Individual manuscript conferencing: yes

Agents/editors attend: yes; *Available for conferencing:* yes

Enrollment: 200-250; *Enrollment limit:* 300

Ancillary activities: contests in the novel, short fiction and poetry; write or call for details

FLORIDA ROMANCE WRITERS ANNUAL CONFERENCE

2000 No. Congress Avenue, #6
West Palm Beach, FL 33409
tel: (407) 684-3651

A weekend conference sponsored by a chapter of Romance Writers of America where "classes are offered in all phases of writing romantic and/or women's fiction. Attendees can request appointments with editors or agents, on a first-received, first-assigned basis."

Director/Contact: Susan McConnell Koski, President

Location(s): Fort Lauderdale, FL

Dates: last weekend in February, 1996

Commenced: 1986

Recent faculty/lecturers: Beatrice Small, Eileen Dreyer, Barbara Bretton, Judy Cuevas, Teresa Medeiros, Dawn E. Reno, Ellen Taber, Becky Lee Weyrich

Marketing guidance: yes

Agents/editors attend: yes; *Available for conferencing:* yes

Enrollment: 200

Ancillary activities: book signings, "Ultimate Pajama Party"

FLORIDA SUNCOAST WRITERS' CONFERENCE
Department of English
University of South Florida
5202 E. Fowler Avenue
Tampa, FL 33260
tel: (813) 974-1711
fax: (813) 974-2270

"A three-day conference which includes over 50 workshops in the short story, nonfiction, mystery and suspense fiction, science fiction, article writing, children's and young adult literature. Features approximately 25 nationally and regionally established writers, agents, editors and publishers."

Director/Contact: Steve Rubin, Edgar Hirschberg, Co-Directors

Location(s): University of South Florida, S. Petersburg Campus, FL.

Dates: first weekend in February, 1996

Commenced: 1971

Recent faculty/lecturers: Edward Albee, Maxine Kumin, Peter Matthiessen, Sharon Olds, Sonia Sanchez, Rosellen Brown, Tim O'Brien

Individual manuscript conferencing: yes; *Editing assistance:* yes; *Marketing guidance:* yes

Agents/editors attend: yes; *Available for conferencing:* yes

Enrollment: 400

Scholarships: available for University of South Florida students only; call or write office above

Ancillary activities: readings, open poetry, brown-bag lunch with a featured writer

KEY WEST LITERARY SEMINAR & WRITERS' WORKSHOP

419 Petronia Street
Key West, FL 33040
tel: (305) 293-9291
fax: (305) 293-0482

A four day conference where "a different topic is selected each year for a seminar and writing workshop. 1996's theme is Nature Writing. Past topics include Journalism, Biography & Autobiography, Travel Writing, writing for the stage and screen, and the work of Elizabeth Bishop, Tennessee Williams & Ernest Hemingway." Both fiction and nonfiction will be addressed in the workshop.

Director/Contact: Monica Haskell, Executive Director

Location(s): Key West, FL

Dates: January 11-14, 1996

Commenced: 1982

Recent faculty/lecturers: David McCullough, Anna Quindlen, Jan Morris, Elmore Leonard, Octavio Paz, Alice Quinn, John Wideman, Peter Matthiessen

Manuscripts: required for workshop only; *Individual manuscript conferencing:* workshop only; *Editing assistance:* workshop only; *Marketing guidance:* workshop only

Agents/editors attend: yes

Enrollment: 350 in seminar, 35 in workshop; *Enrollment limit:* 35 in workshop

Ancillary activities: literary walking tours, book signings, receptions, dedications

KEY WEST LITERARY SEMINAR WRITERS' WORKSHOPS

410 Caroline Street
Key West, FL 33040
tel: (305) 296-3573
fax: (305) 293-0482

Three workshops covering seven days each in fiction, short story and poetry. "Classes and group discussions are held in the mornings. The afternoons are reserved for private consultations."

Director/Contact: Judith Gaddis

Location(s): Heritage House Museum, Key West, FL

Dates: February (fiction), March (poetry), April (short story), 1996

Commenced: 1995

Recent faculty/lecturers: Mary Lee Settle, Phyllis Janowitz, Roxana Robinson

Manuscripts: required; *Individual manuscript conferencing:* yes

Enrollment: 10 registrants per workshop—admission based upon quality of submitted manuscripts

Ancillary activities: literary walking tours, book signings, receptions, sunset readings

SPACE COAST WRITERS' GUILD INC. CONFERENCE
Box 804
Melbourne, FL 32902
tel: (407) 727-0051

A "balanced two-day program preparing oneself and one's work for the writing world." The writers' conference offers numerous workshops, including "building plot, setting and characterization," "creating fiction, developing dialogue and building tension," "writing and marketing your short story," "your children's book: communicating by seeing through the eyes of your readers."

Director/Contact: Dr. Edwin J. Kirschner, President

Location (s): Cocoa Beach, FL

Dates: First Friday-Saturday in November, 1996

Commenced: 1981

Recent faculty/lecturers: Kirk Polking, Kenneth Thurston, Ben Bova, Lynn Armisted McKee, James W. Hall, Gabriel Horn

Individual manuscript conferencing: no individual help, but the conference program offers general editing assistance and marketing guidance

Agents/editors attend: yes

Enrollment: 340; *Enrollment limit:* 340

Scholarships: yes, to a local college student selected by the instructors

Ancillary activities: conference writing contests (book manuscript, short story, poetry, short story for children, short play, feature article); year-round membership activities

GEORGIA

AMERICAN CHRISTIAN WRITERS CONFERENCE
(held in Atlanta, GA, October, 1996 see Arizona for details)

CURRY HILL PLANTATION WRITERS' RETREAT
(held in Bainbridge GA, March, April, 1996—
see Mississippi for details)

MOONLIGHT & MAGNOLIAS WRITERS' CONFERENCE
4378 Karls Gate Drive
Marietta, GA 30068
tel: (404) 973-6162
fax: (404) 977-2707

A weekend conference on women's fiction, sponsored by the Georgia Romance Writers (a chapter of the Romance Writers of America) and offering "a choice of 30 workshops, many of which are geared toward writing in general (not just romance)." Also offering "small, hands-on sessions/workshops for new writers," published or non-published.

Director/Contact: Carol Springston, Coordinator

Location(s): Doubletree Hotel, Atlanta, GA

Dates: Third weekend in September, 1996

Commenced: 1981

Recent faculty/lecturers: Judith McNaught, Sandra Brown, Deborah Smith, Patricia Potter, Sandra Chastain, Nan Ryan, Heather Graham, Nora Roberts

Individual manuscript conferencing: no, but there could be group conferencing; *Marketing guidance:* yes

Agents/editors attend: yes; *Available for conferencing:* yes

Enrollment: 300

Ancillary activities: "Maggie" contest for both published and unpublished writers; special workshops on last day with judges critiquing specific manuscripts

SOUTHEASTERN WRITERS' CONFERENCE
Route 1, Box 102
Cuthbert, GA 31740
tel: (912) 679-5445

This conference runs for several days and is appropriate for all writing levels. The program covers "fiction, nonfiction, poetry, play writing, mass market and juvenile" work.

Director/Contact: Pat Laye, Co-Director

Location(s): St. Simons Island, GA

Dates: June, 1996

Commenced: 1974

Recent faculty/lecturers: Carol Ippolito, Nancy McKnight, Nelle McFather, Leroy Spruill, Memye Curtis Tucker

Individual manuscript conferencing: yes; *Marketing guidance:* yes

Agents/editors attend: yes

Enrollment: 100; *Enrollment limit:* 100

Scholarships: two are available for young writers

Ancillary activities: several contests with money prizes for manuscripts entered by registered attendees

HAWAII

MAUI WRITERS' CONFERENCE
P.O. Box 10307
Lahaina, HI 96761
tel/fax: (808) 669-6109

4-day conference (including pre-conference special workshops) covering "fiction, nonfiction, poetry, screenwriting/ films." Recent conferences have included travel writing, magazine writing, Hawaiiana and multi-media interactive writing. But "our program changes slightly from year to year."

Director/Contact: John Tullius, Director; Shannon Tullius, Executive Director

Location(s): uncertain for 1996; 1995 at The Grand Wailea Resort and Spa, Maui

Dates: August 30-31, September 1-2, 1996

Commenced: 1993

Recent faculty/lecturers: Bryce Courtenay, Dan Millman, W.S. Merwin, Terry Anderson, Shane Black, Joe Eszterhas, Richard Walter, Dr. Susan Forward

Individual manuscript conferencing: yes; *Marketing guidance:* yes

Agents/editors attend: yes; *Available for conferencing:* yes

Enrollment: 500-600

Scholarships: winner of *The Forum-Screenwrite Now!* magazine contest receives free lodging and airfare; Hawaiian high school student winner of Hawaiian-theme essay contest receives full assistance and free airfare

Ancillary activities: Sunset Bar-B-Q on the Beach

ILLINOIS

CHRISTIAN WRITER'S INSTITUTE
(held in Wheaton, IL, June, 1996, see Florida for details)

MISSISSIPPI VALLEY WRITERS' CONFERENCE
Union Building
Augustana College
Rock Island, IL 61201
tel: (309) 762-8985

Nine one-hour workshops are offered daily "in the areas of beginning professional writing, poetry, juveniles, nonfiction, writing romantic fiction, novel/basics, short story, novel manuscript seminar and photography."

Director/Contact: David R. Collins, Director

Location(s): campus of Augustana College, Rock Island, IL

Dates: June 2-7, 1996

Commenced: 1973

Recent faculty/lecturers: Max Collins, Karl Largent, Evelyn Witter, Connie Heckert, Dick Stahl, Rich Johnson, Roald Tweet, David McFarland, Kim Bush. H.E. Francis

Manuscripts: required for novel manuscript seminar workshop;
  Individual manuscript conferencing: yes; *Marketing guidance:* yes

Enrollment: 80

Ancillary activities: cash awards for submitted manuscripts; awards banquet; nightly events feature readings, etc.

INDIANA

❧

INDIANA UNIVERSITY WRITERS' CONFERENCE
Ballantine 464
Indiana University
Bloomington, IN 47405
tel: (812) 855-1877

The conference "offers both classes and workshops. Week-long workshops foster close working relationships between teachers and workshop members, ensuring that conferees are given extensive advice and encouragement in their writing." There are three workshops in fiction, three in poetry and one in nonfiction, "as well as classes and seminars."

Director/Contact: Sascha Feinstein, Director

Location(s): Indiana Memorial Union and other buildings on the Indiana University campus

Dates: June 23-28, 1996

Commenced: 1940

Recent faculty/lecturers: William Mathews, Richard Yates, Susan Dodd, Heather McHugh, Robert Boswell, Joan Silber, Garret Hongo, Ellen Bryant Voight

Manuscript: required; *Individual manuscript conferencing:* yes; *Marketing guidance:* yes, by means of general seminar only *Editors attend:* yes, but not available for conferencing

Enrollment: 110; *Enrollment limit:* 110-120

Scholarships: available; all conference applicants automatically considered, no special application required

Ancillary activities: readings by staff and by those attending the conference

Midwest Writers' Workshop

Dept. of Journalism
Ball State University
Muncie, IN 47306
tel: (317) 285-8200
fax: (317) 285-7997

A four-day series of workshops covering "fiction, nonfiction, poetry and selected special areas plus evening speakers, 'talkabouts' and special sessions. Editor-in-residence and agent-in-residence for conferences plus manuscript evaluations."

Director/Contact: Earl L. Conn, Director

Location(s): Hotel Roberts, Muncie, IN

Dates: July 24-27, 1996

Commenced: 1972

Recent faculty/lecturers: William Zinsser, Dennis Hensley, Peter Jacobi, Alice Friman, Bill Myers, Rita Berman, Lee Pennington, Virginia Muir, Alan Seaburg

Individual manuscript conferencing: yes; *Marketing guidance:* yes

Agents/editors attend: yes; *Available for conferencing:* yes

Enrollment: 125

Scholarships: 10 are available. Send letter of application, writing sample to Scholarship Committee

Ropewalk Writer's Retreat
English Dept.
University of Southern Indiana
Evansville, IN 47712
tel: (812) 464-1953

"A week-long conference with workshops dealing with poetry, fiction and nonfiction. Also, the conference allows time to write."

Director/Contact: Mathew Graham

Location: New Harmony, IN

Dates: mid-June, 1996

Commenced: 1988

Recent faculty/lecturers: Phil Levine, Joy Williams, Ann Beattie, Larry Levis, Heather McHugh, Amy Hemple

Manuscript: required; *Individual manuscript conferencing:* yes

Enrollment: 40-50; *Enrollment limit:* 60

Scholarships: yes, contact English Department

Ancillary activities: readings by faculty each evening

IOWA

CHILDREN'S PICTURE BOOK SEMINAR
Scott Community College
500 Belmont Road
Bettendorf, IA 52722
tel: (319) 359-7531
fax: (319) 359-0519

A one-day seminar "for persons interested in writing a children's picture book. Morning session is devoted to discussing techniques and procedures for writing, illustrating and marketing... The afternoon is devoted to hands-on activities on participants manuscripts."

Director/Contact: Betty Smith, Community Education

Location(s): Scott Community College Urban Center, Davenport, IA

Dates: uncertain (1995 seminar, August, 1995)

Commenced: 1987

Recent faculty/lecturers: Peter Davidson

Individual manuscript conferencing: yes; *Editing assistance:* yes; *Marketing guidance:* yes

Enrollment limit: 60

IOWA SUMMER WRITING FESTIVAL
116 International Center
University of Iowa
Iowa City, Iowa 52242
tel: (319) 335-2534 • *fax:* (319) 335-2740

Weeklong or weekend "workshops in fiction, nonfiction, poetry, essay, film writing for children, romance, mystery and more with 12 per class and 100 classes offered."

Director/Contact: Peggy Houston, Director

Location(s): Iowa City, Iowa

Dates: June 9-July 27, 1996

Commenced: 1987

Recent faculty/lecturers: W.P. Kinsella, Robert Olen Butler, Robert Waller, Hope Edelman, Mona Van Dynn

Individual manuscript conferencing: yes

Enrollment: 1000—no enrollment limit

Ancillary activities: weekly readings by renowned writers

SINIPEE WRITERS' WORKSHOP
P.O. Box 902
Dubuque, Iowa 52004-0902
tel: (319) 556-0366

One-day workshop where "all forms of writing are addressed: fiction (both short story and novel); all nonfiction; poetry; play writing etc."

Director/Contact: John Tigges, Director

Location(s): campus of Clark College, Dubuque, Iowa

Dates: April 20, 1996

Commenced: 1985

Recent faculty/lecturers: Dick Locher, David Rabe, Tom Gifford, Robert Byrne, Ben Logan, Kay McMahon

Editing assistance: yes

Agents/editors attend: yes; *Available for conferencing:* yes

Enrollment: 50-150

Scholarships: up to 50% reduction available; send student status or senior-citizen status with application

Ancillary activities: contests for short fiction (1500 words or less), poetry (40 lines or less), nonfiction/article (1500 words or less)

KANSAS

WRITERS' WORKSHOP IN SCIENCE FICTION

English Department
University of Kansas
Lawrence, KS 66045
tel: (913) 874-3380
fax: (913) 864-4298

A two-week conference with workshops in science fiction (and some fantasy) "aiming at publication; three stories are required before the start of the workshop; one is revised over the first weekend; guest writers and editors."

Director/Contact: Professor James Gunn

Location(s): campus of University of Kansas, Lawrence, KS

Dates: June 26-July 9, 1996

Commenced: 1985

Recent faculty/lecturers: Frederik Pohl, John Ordover, Kij Johnson, James Gunn

Manuscript: required; *Individual manuscript conferencing:* yes; *Editing assistance:* yes; *Marketing guidance:* yes

Agents/editors attend: yes; *Available for conferencing:* yes

Enrollment: 10; *Enrollment limit:* 15

Ancillary activities: The Campbell Conference (a round-table discussion of issues in science fiction publishing, writing and teaching); Campbell and Sturgeon Awards presentations

KENTUCKY

GREEN RIVER WRITER'S RETREAT
11906 Locust Road
Middletown, KY 40243
tel: (502) 245-4902

"A weekend of workshops (small-medium groups) with emphasis on fiction, poetry, essay, followed by a week of Retreat during which participants read, write, critique each other's work. Retreat week is entirely participant led and oriented."

Director/Contact: Mary E. O'Dell, Director

Location(s): Louisville, KY

Dates: 3rd week of July, 1996

Commenced: 1984

Recent faculty/lecturers: Jim W. Miller, Lee Pennington, George Ella Lyon

Individual manuscript conferencing: yes; *Editing assistance:* yes; *Marketing guidance:* yes

Enrollment: 50; *Enrollment limit:* 50-60

Novels-in-Progress Workshop
208 La Fontenay
Louisville, KY 40223
tel: (502) 244-0857

Sponsored by the Green River Writers, this is a "five-day workshop consisting of small group classes (2 hours, 5-6 participants each) with novelist instructors; weekend following is for agent/editor activities and interaction with participants."

Director/Contact: Sandra Daugherty

Location(s): Louisville, KY

Dates: first week of January, 1996

Commenced: 1990

Recent faculty/lecturers: Bob Mayer, Lynn Hightower, Steve Womack, Terence Faherty, Karen Field, Gary Devon

Manuscripts: partial sample required; *Individual manuscript conferencing:* yes; *Editing assistance:* yes; *Marketing guidance:* yes

Agents/editors attend: yes; *Available for conferencing:* yes

Enrollment: 35; *Enrollment limit:* 40 plus

Scholarships: yes, call or write

Ancillary activities: participants are free to audit any classes they wish; Green River Writers' motto is: *Writers Helping Writers*

LOUISIANA

DEEP SOUTH WRITERS' CONFERENCE

English Department, University of Southwestern Louisiana
P.O. Box 44691, USL Station
Lafayette, LA 70504
tel: (318) 482-6918

A three-day conference "interested in all genres that fit under the general creative-writing rubric [fiction, nonfiction, poetry, play writing etc.]. Its principal aim is to encourage new writers and provide a context of collegiality for more experienced ones." Both general and special workshops are offered.

Director/Contact: Dr. John W. Fiero, Director; Dr. Wendell Mayo, Program Chair

Location(s): campus of Univeristy of Southwestern Louisiana

Dates: September 27-29, 1996

Commenced: 1960

Recent faculty/lecturers: Robert Olen Butler, Siv Cedering, Ernest Gaines, Janet Burroway, Edward Hirsch, Ellen Gilchrist, Tony Fenneley, Robert Haas

Manuscripts: required only for special workshops; *Individual manuscript conferencing:* for workshop registrants

Agents/editors attend: yes; not usually available for conferencing

Enrollment: 200; *Enrollment limit:* 10-12 per workshop, by special subscription

Ancillary activities: readings, an annual contest and publication of The Chapbook, an anthology of prize-winning and honorable mention works from each year's contest

MAINE

STATE OF MAINE WRITERS' CONFERENCE

P.O. Box 146
Ocean Park, ME 04063-0146
tel: (413) 596-6734

A three-day conference, "eclectic—a little bit of everything—emphasis on poetry, children's and religious writing."

Director/Contact: Richard F. Burns, Chairman

Location(s): Ocean Park, ME

Dates: August 20-23, 1996

Commenced: 1941

Recent faculty/lecturers: Roger MacBride, David McCord

Marketing guidance: sometimes

Agents/editors attend: yes

Enrollment: 30-60—no enrollment limit

Ancillary activities: writing contests open to conferees

MARYLAND

AMERICAN MEDICAL WRITERS ASSOCIATION ANNUAL CONFERENCE

9650 Rockville Pike
Bethesda, MD 20814-3998
tel: (301) 493-0003
fax: (301) 493-6384

A three-day conference with nonfiction workshops set
up to improve biomedical-communications skills for the medical
communicator in audiovisual, editing/writing, education, freelance,
pharmaceutical and public relations specialities.

Director/Contact: Lillian Sablack, Executive Director

Location(s): major hotel in Chicago, Illinois

Dates: November 6-9, 1996

Commenced: 1940

Enrollment: 650-700; *Enrollment limit:* vary from workshop to
workshop

Ancillary activities: creative-reading session, banquet and
membership dinner, President's reception, award luncheons

THE LITERARY FESTIVAL AT ST. MARY'S COLLEGE
St. Mary's College of Maryland
St. Mary's City, MD 20686
tel: (301) 862-0239
fax: (301) 862-0958

A two-week conference with morning and afternoon workshop sessions in fiction and poetry during the week. On weekends, "students will actively participate in the 1996 Literary Festitval at St. Mary's, led by guest writers [and] composed of readings, workshops and seminars and lecture/demonstrations."

Director/Contact: Michael Glaser, Montgomery Hall 122

Location(s): campus of St. Mary's College. St. Mary's City, MD

Dates: May 15-28, 1996

Commenced: 1979

Recent faculty/lecturers: Lucille Clifton, Bruce Weigl, Maria Mazziotti Gillan, Jean Nordhaus, Roland Flint, Minnie Bruce Dratt, Ann Darr, Maxine Claire, Rubin Jackson

Manuscript: required; *Individual manuscript conferencing:* yes; *Editing assistance:* yes; *Marketing guidance:* yes

Enrollment: 200; *Enrollment limit:* 15 per workshop

Ancillary activities: readings

MASSACHUSETTS

MOUNT HOLYOKE WRITERS' CONFERENCE
P.O. Box 3213N
Mount Holyoke College
South Hadley, MA 01075
tel: (413) 538-2308
fax: (413) 538-2138

A nine-day workshop program covering fiction, nonfiction and poetry. There are afternoon fiction, nonfiction and poetry workshops as well as craft presentations and panels. In the mornings, students write and confer.

Director/Contact: Michael Pettit, Director

Location(s): campus of Mt. Holyoke College, South Hadley, MA

Dates: mid-late June, 1996

Commenced: 1988

Recent faculty/lecturers: Galway Kinnell, Peter Matthiessen, Tracey Kidder, Nancy Willard, Stephan Dobyns

Manuscripts: required; *Individual manuscript conferencing:* yes; *Editing assistance:* yes; *Marketing guidance:* yes

Agents/editors attend: yes; *Available for conferencing:* yes

Enrollment: 75; *Enrollment limit:* 15 per workshop

Scholarships: yes, apply with manuscript and one page narrative statement of need

Ancillary activities: readings, book-signing parties, barbeques

NEW ENGLAND WRITERS' WORKSHOP AT SIMMONS COLLEGE

300 The Fenway
Boston, MA 02115
tel: (617) 521-2090
fax: (617) 521-3199

A five-day workshop where "professional and aspiring writers assess each other's work and explore the problems and rewards of writing for publication. Participants work in adult fiction: novels and short stories. The groups meet in morning classes and in the afternoons with workshop leaders for discussion, evaluation and criticism of manuscripts."

Director/Contact: C. Michael Curtis, Director, Jean Chaput Welch, Ass't Director

Location(s): Simmons College, Boston MA

Dates: early June, 1996

Commenced: 1978

Recent faculty/lecturers: Sue Miller, Ralph Lombreglia, John Updike, Stephan King, Robert Parker, Ann Beattie

Manuscripts: not required but will be reviewed if submitted; *Individual manuscript conferencing:* yes; *Editing assistance:* yes; *Marketing guidance:* yes

Agents/editors attend: yes; *Available for conferencing:* yes

Enrollment: 45

Ancillary activities: workshop staff readings, participant readings

PERSPECTIVES IN CHILDREN'S LITERATURE CONFERENCE

226 Furcolo Hall
University of Massachusetts
Amherst, MA 01003-3035
tel: (413) 545-4325
fax: (413) 545-2879

A one-day conference consisting of "presentations of fiction, nonfiction, poetry etc. by both authors and illustrators. It is attended by teachers, librarians, writers, illustrators, parents and students."

Director/Contact: Dr. Masha Rudman, Director

Location(s): campus of University of Massachusetts at Amherst, MA

Dates: April 27, 1996

Commenced: 1960

Recent faculty/lecturers: Elilzabeth Howard, Katherine Patterson, Barry Moser, Patricia MacLachlan, Liza Ketchum Murrow, Elizabeth Gordon, Irene Hector-Smalls, James Ransome

Agents/editors attend: yes

Enrollment: 500; *Enrollment limit:* 500

Ancillary activities: book sale, exhibits, door prizes

MICHIGAN

AMERICAN CHRISTIAN WRITERS CONFERENCE
(held June, 1996 in Detroit, Michigan. See Arizona for details)

CLARION SCIENCE FICTION AND FANTASY WRITERS' WORKSHOP
Lyman Briggs School,
Michigan State University
E-185 Holmes Hall
East Lansing, MI 48825-1107
tel: (517) 355-9598
fax: (517) 353-4765

A six-week series of workshops focusing on science fiction and fantasy short stories. "Each week a different professional writer conducts the workshop. Mornings are devoted to analyzing manuscripts in in a workshop setting; afternoons and evenings are devoted to individual writing, conferences with the writer in residence, and completing class assignments."

Director/Contact: Tess Tavormina, Director; Mary Sheridan, Coordinator

Location(s): campus of Michigan State University, East Lansing, MI

Dates: mid-June, early August, 1996

Commenced: 1968

Recent faculty/lecturers: Damon Knight, Kate Wilhelm, Samuel R. Delany, Karen Joy Fowler, Tim Powers, Joe Haldeman, Nancy Kress, Kim Stanley Robinson

Manuscripts: required; *Individual manuscript conferencing:* yes; *Editing assistance:* yes; *Marketing guidance:* yes

Agents/editors attend: yes; *Available for conferencing:* sometimes

Enrollment: 18; *Enrollment limit:* 25

Scholarships: yes

Ancillary activities: signings and readings by writers-in-residence; newsletters for alumni; e-mail listserver network for alumni

MIDLAND WRITERS' CONFERENCE
Grace A. Dow Memorial Library
1710 W. St. Andrews
Midland, MI 48640
tel: (517) 835-7151
fax: (517) 835-9791

One-day conference "composed of a well-known keynote speaker, followed by six workshops on a variety of subjects, including poetry, writing for children, fiction writing, news reporting."

Director/Contact: Barbara S. Brennan, Coordinator

Location(s): Grace A. Dow Memorial Library auditorium and conference rooms

Dates: 2nd Saturday in June, 1996

Commenced: 1980

Recent faculty/lecturers: P.J. O'Rourke, Andrew Greeley, Mary Higgins Clark, Kurt Vonnegut, Joseph Heller

Marketing guidance: yes

Enrollment: 100

OAKLAND UNIVERSITY AND DETROIT WOMEN WRITERS ANNUAL WRITERS' CONFERENCE

Continuing Eduucation
265 SFH
Oakland University
Rochester, MI 48309-4401
tel: (810) 370-3120
fax: (810) 370-3137

A two-day conference co-sponsored by Oakland University and the Detroit Women Writers with "36 concurrent sessions on topics of interest to beginning through published writers." One-on-one and workshop critiques are conducted by authors, publishers and agents and covered are fiction (including genres such as mysteries, science fiction), nonfiction, poetry, essays, children's literature, play writing.

Director/Contact: Nadine Jakobowski, Director

Location(s): campus of Oakland University, Rochester, MI

Dates: October, 1996

Commenced: 1961

Recent faculty/lecturers: Dutch Leonard, Loren Estleman, Margaret Hillert, William Kienzel, Shelby Hearon, William Zinsser

Individual manuscript conferencing: yes; *Editing assistance:* yes; *Marketing guidance:* yes

Agents/editors attend: yes—and conduct workshops

Enrollment: 450; *Enrollment limit:* only by size of room

Scholarships: yes, but only to undergraduate and graduate students in Michigan educational institutions

MINNESOTA

AMERICAN CHRISTIAN WRITERS CONFERENCE
(held August, 1996 in Minneapolis, MN, see Arizona for details)

HOW TO WRITE CHILDREN'S PICTURE BOOKS AND WRITER'S SEMINAR
Lakewood Community College
Continuing Education
3401 Century Avenue
White Bear Lake, MN 55110
tel: (612) 779-3341
fax: (612) 779-3417

These are two workshops, each one day in length. For children's picture books "the morning will be devoted to discussing techniques and procedures for writing and marketing. The afternoon will be devoted to hands-on activities and to working on participants' manuscripts." The Writer's Seminar "is for anyone interested in writing magazine articles, short stories, children's books, fiction, nonfiction, textbooks, religious works, poetry, songs."

Director/Contact: Pat Lockyear, Director, Community Education

Location(s): Lakewood Community College, White Bear Lake, MN

Dates: Writer's Seminar—spring quarter, 1996
Children's Picture Books—fall quarter, 1996

Commenced: 1991

Recent faculty/lecturers: Peter Davidson

Individual manuscript conferencing: yes; *Editing assistance:* yes;
Marketing guidance: yes

Enrollment: 20-30

MISSISSIPPI RIVER CREATIVE WRITING WORKSHOP
St. Cloud University
St. Cloud, MN 56303
tel: (612) 255-3061

A two week workshop (and college credit undergraduate and graduate course) in fiction and poetry; "the first week will include discussions of poetry and fiction-writing techniques; during the second week, one published writer will visit each day to discuss his/her writing and to answer questions concerning writing techniques."

Director/Contact: William Meissner

Location(s): campus of St. Cloud University, St. Cloud, MN

Dates: June, 1996

Commenced: 1973

Recent faculty/lecturers: Kate Green, Michael Dennis Brown, Margaret Hasse, Leonard Witt, Bill Meissner

Enrollment: 35

SPLIT ROCK ARTS PROGRAM, UNIVERSITY OF MINNESOTA
306 Wesbrook Hall
77 Pleasant St. SE
Minneapolis, MN 55455
tel: (612) 624-6800
fax: (612) 624-5891

"Intensive one-week residential workshops in writing, visual arts, fine crafts and enhancement of creativity. Writing workshops include, fiction, nonfiction, poetry and children's literature."

Director/Contact: Phyllis Campbell, Program Associate

Location(s): Duluth campus of University of Minnnesota

Dates: July 7-August 10, 1996

Commenced: 1983

Recent faculty/lecturers: Marion Dane Bauer, Richard Bausch, Carolyn Forche, Mark Harris, Jane Howard, Al Young, Valerie Miner, Mikhail Iossel, Sandra Benitez

Individual manuscript conferencing: varies; *Editing assistance:* varies; *Marketing guidance:* varies

Enrollment: 600 per season; *Enrollment limit:* 16 per class

Scholarships: yes, see catalogue for instructions

"WRITING TO SELL" CONFERENCE
Writers' Workshop Conference Director
P.O. Box 24356
Minneapolis, MN 55424

A two-day annual conference sponsored by a nonprofit organization that has been holding weekly meetings for writers since was established in 1937. All work is done by volunteers, and at each conference 10-12 writers, editors, publishers are featured, along with an agent or editor from New York. "But most of our speakers come from the vast publishing community located in Minneapolis-St. Paul."

Director/Contact: Herb Montgomery (612-922-0724)

Location(s): downtown Minneapolis, MN hotel

Dates: August 10-11, 1996

Commenced: 1985

Recent faculty/lecturers: R.D. Zimmerman, Marion Dane Bauer

Marketing guidance: yes

Agents/editor attend: yes

Enrollment: 100-125; *Enrollment limit:* none

Ancilary activities: literary contest with emphasis on recognizing "promising writers"

MISSISSIPPI

CURRY HILL PLANTATION WRITER'S RETREAT

404 Crestmont Avenue

Hattiesburg, MS 39401

tel: (601) 264-7034

or

P.O. Box 514

Bainbridge, GA 31717

tel: (912) 246-3369

This one-week writer's retreat, offered twice in the spring, covers fiction and nonfiction only, and is "an opportunity for a select group of serious writers to advance their talents by group discussion of their work, plus individual professional consultation."

Director/Contact: Elizabeth Browne

Location(s): Curry Hill Plantation, an ante-bellum estate on 400 acres, near Bainbridge, Georgia

Dates: one week each, March, April, 1996

Commenced: 1977

Recent faculty/lecturers: Elizabeth Browne

Individual manuscript conferencing: yes; *Editing assistance:* yes; *Marketing guidance:* yes

Enrollment: 6-8 at each session; *Enrollment limit:* 6-8 per session

MISSOURI

American Christian Writers Conference

(held June, 1996 in St. Louis, MO. See AZ for details)

Fiction from the Heartland Conference

P.O. Box 32186
Kansas City, MO 64111
tel: (913) 856-8521
fax: (913) 856-8521

Sponsored by the Mid-America Romance Authors, this weekend conference focuses on "genre and popular book-length fiction. Program includes keynote and special guest speakers, editors, agents and authors in 16 to 20 workshops, question and answer panels."

Director/Contact: Conference Director

Location(s): Kansas City, MO

Dates: February 9-11, 1996

Commenced: 1988

Recent faculty/lecturers: Julie Garwood, Jill Barnett, Karen Robards, Constance O'Day Flannery

Editing assistance: yes; *Marketing guidance:* yes

Agents/editors attend: yes; *Available for conferencing:* yes

Enrollment: 150-200

Ancillary activities: book signings with over 25 authors; fiction contest

MARK TWAIN WRITERS' CONFERENCE
921 Center Street
Hannibal, MO 63401
tel: (800) 747-0738
fax: (314) 221-6409

Sponsored by Hannibal-LaGrange College for undergraduate credit and University of Missouri, Kirksville, for graduate credit, this conference offers workshops in many writing areas, including humor, magazine writing, short story, full-length fiction, general nonfiction, children's literature and poetry.

Director/Contact: James C. Hefley, Director, Cyni Allison, Coordinator

Location (s): Hannibal-LaGrange College campus, Hannibal, MO

Dates: lst week in June, 1996

Commenced: 1985

Recent faculty/lecturers: Gene Perret, Bruce Woods, Michael Bugeta, Sue Monk Kidd, Jerry Jenkins, Cliff Schimmels

Individual manuscript conferencing: yes; *Editing assistance:* yes; *Marketing guidance:* yes

Agents/editors attend: yes; *Available for conferencing:* yes

Enrollment: 125; *Enrollment limit:* 125

NEW HAMPSHIREANNUAL FESTIVAL OF POETRY AT THE FROST PLACE

The Frost Place
Franconia, NH 03580
tel: (603) 823-5510

A seven-day conference "for poets: daily seminars, readings and organized critique of participant work and private conferences." Poetry only, small workshops (6-8 participants), "each day of the Festival is presided over by one of the six nationally known poets invited as Guest Faculty."

Director/Contact: Donald Sheehan, Executive Director

Location(s): The Frost Place, Franconia, NH

Dates: August 4-10, 1996

Commenced: 1979

Recent faculty/lecturers: Donald Hall, Molly Peacock, Martin Espada, Dana Gioia, William Mathews, Nicholas Samaras

Manuscript: required—3 pages of poetry; *Individual manuscript conferencing:* yes; *Editing assistance:* yes; *Marketing guidance:* yes

Enrollment: 45; *Enrollment limit:* 45

Scholarships: no, but budget-tuition payments are possible

Ancillary activities: readings by faculty and participants

NEW JERSEY

TRENTON STATE COLLEGE WRITERS' CONFERENCE

Trenton State College
English Dept.
Hillwood Lakes 4700
Trenton, NJ 08650-4700
tel: (609) 771-3254

"A day of readings, workshops and panels with literary agents, editors and noted authors in fiction, nonfiction, play writing, television, screenwriting, poetry; literature for the young; magazine and newspaper journalism." A separate workshop on writer's-block busting is also offered.

Director/Contact: Jean Hollander, Director

Location(s): Brower Student center, campus of Trenton State College, Trenton, NJ

Dates: April, 1996

Commenced: 1981

Recent faculty/lecturers: Kurt Vonnegut, Arthur Miller, Toni Morrison, Erica Jong, Edward Albee, Robert Kaplow, Laura Boss, Thomas William Simpson, Richard Burgin, Laura Cunningham, Edwin Romond

Individual manuscript conferencing: yes; *Editing assistance:* yes; *Marketing guidance:* yes

Agents/editors attend: yes

Enrollment: 700; *Enrollment limit:* for some workshops

Scholarships: none directly, but lower student rates are offered

Ancillary activities: fiction and poetry contests, readings

THE WRITERS FOR RACING PROJECT

P.O. Box 3098
Princeton, NJ 08543-3098
tel: (609) 275-2947
fax: (609) 275-1243

A two-week workshop at three separate locations that "brings creative writers in any genre into the diverse environment of the racehorse. It provides a structured academic settlement for university students and writers within the greater horse industry, as well." Covered are fiction, creative nonfiction and poetry.

Director/Contact: Karl Garson

Location(s): (1) Churchill Downs, Louisville, KY, (2) A Western or West Coast racetrack (3) an East Coast racetrack

Dates: (1) June 9-23, 1996, (2) July 7-21, 1996, (3) July 28-August 11, 1996

Commenced: 1992

Recent faculty/lecturers: Lee K. Abbott, Gerald Costanzo, Gary Gildner, Jana Harris, Teresa J. Hordan, William Pitt Root, Pamela Uschuk, Irene Wanner, Paul Zarzyski, Paul Zimmer

Manuscripts: required; *Individual manuscript conferencing:* yes; *Editing assistance:* yes; *Marketing guidance:* yes

Agents/Editors attend: yes; *Available for Conferencing:* yes

Enrollment: 10-15 per workshop; *Enrollment limit:* 15 per workshop

Scholarships: yes

Ancillary activities: faculty readings, student readings, directors' awards

MEET... KARL GARSON

DIRECTOR, WRITERS FOR RACING PROJECT

F OR MANY OF US the thrill of horseracing begins and ends with a televised spectacle. But, according to Karl Garson, the sport is definitely underexposed, even with mega awards and a coterie of firmly dedicated partisans. The reason? There simply isn't enough good writing about horses and horseracing to lure a larger audience.

"You aren't going to get sports page editors interested," Garson, Director of the Writers for Racing Project, says. He cites a recent study which surveyed sports' editors attitudes toward horseracing. "Almost universally the editors thought no one cared about horseracing," and that translated into what appeared on their pages." In the survey, however, the public showed they cared about the horse *industry*, but there didn't seem any way to convince the editors the public wanted more news about horseracing."

Garson, one-time columnist and feature writer for *The Daily Racing Form,* had an idea. "In watching the writing about thoroughbred and quarter horse racing in other papers and magazines, I came to realize that writing about the horse could be improved, so I decided to approach it from the creative-writing point of view." Trying to write for the sports pages, he knew, was hopeless, especially with the sports editors' biases. "You're better off trying to get into quality print, small press, quality fiction, quality poetry," and to develop stories and poetry around the theme of the horse.

In May, 1993 he left *The Daily Racing Form*, acquired funding from thoroughbred and quarter horse racing and breeding organizations and set in motion a plan he had been working on for more than a year. He would develop writers' workshops geared to creative writing about the horse, *he would hold these workshops at or close to major horseracing tracks* and he would expose his students to all nearby horse-related activity!

Garson has credentials: he's taught creative writing and English at three different universities, and he's been well published. "I said to myself, there's a better way to go about this, and it's through creative writing. So I hired a faculty, and I recruited students through the traditional creative-writing venues such as *Poets and Writers, AWP Chronicle*—and the only difference is that the workshops are held at a race track and not in a classroom somewhere."

The workshops run at three different locations during the summer, and the sessions don't overlap. Because the locations change, so does the faculty. In the early summer Garson calls it "The Bluegrass Writers' Workshop," and the location is the home of the Kentucky Derby, Churchill Downs, Louisville, Kentucky. Faculty has included Gary Gildner, Gerald Costanzo and Jim Bolus, official historian of the Kentucky Derby.

Midsummer, the scene will shift out west, perhaps to a race track on the West Coast, and Garson calls it "A Stay at the Races." Memoirist Teresa Jordan joins in, along with cowboy poet Paul Zarzyski.

In late summer, 1996, the program will move east, more than likely to a racetrack on the East Coast. New faculty arrives, too; in the past it has included two-time Pulitzer Prize nominee for poetry, William Pitt Root, two-time Pulitzer Prize nominee for fiction, Lee K. Abbott and poet/fiction writer Pamela Uschuk.

Garson has no trouble filling the workshops; in fact, there have been more applications than places to be filled. "If I had a choice, I'd pick workshop participants who have never seen a horse in their lives," he says. "My ideal is a *tabula rasa*, a bright, creative person who comes to the equation with an absolutely clean slate, no pre-conceived notions." He wants them to drink in the color of the overall horse scene. "I urge people to write about the subject—the track or horses—and I want them to write based on the inspiration that subject gives them." He pauses. "We see horses breed, you know."

Smiling now. "Everyone's fascinated."

NEW MEXICO

TAOS INSTITUTE OF ARTS WORKSHOP
P.O. Box 2469
Taos, NM 87571
tel: (505) 758-2793
fax: (505) 751-0735

"Intensive week-long college-credited workshops in fiction writing; poetry writing; manuscript revision; writing for magazines; the business of writing; the muse of writing; literature of Northern New Mexico."

Director/Contact: Ursula Beck, Director; Joanne Welde, Registrar

Location(s): at local bed-and-breakfast sites

Dates: classes throughout summer and early fall, 1996

Commenced: 1989

Recent faculty/lecturers: Melissa Pritchard, Rudolfo Ahaya, Natalie Goldberg, Jim Sagel, Miriam Sagan, Alexander Blackburn

Manuscripts: required for certain courses; *Editing assistance:* yes; *Marketing guidance:* yes

Agents/editors attend: yes; *Available for conferencing:* yes

Enrollment: 12 per class

Scholarships: yes, for residents of Taos County, NM only

NEW YORK

❁

ASJA Annual Writers' Conference
1501 Broadway #302
New York, NY 10036
tel: (212) 997-0947
fax: (212) 768-7414

Sponsored by the American Society of Journalists and Authors, this weekend conference offers 25 workshops, panel discussions and lectures, mostly on nonfiction, and highlighting marketing and trends in books, magazines, television, video, film etc.

Director/Contact: Alexandra Cantor, Director

Location(s): Sheraton Hotel, New York City, NY

Dates: May weekend, 1996

Commenced: 1971

Recent faculty/lecturers: Anna Quindlen, Brigitte Weeks, William Novak, Mary Higgins Clark

Marketing guidance: yes

Agents/editors attend: yes

Enrollment: 700

Feminist Women's Writing Workshops, Inc
P.O. Box 6583
Ithaca, NY 14851

A one-week program that "includes small-group writing sessions; critique; workshops on a variety of topics; evening readings and talk; workshop participants are encouraged to work in one or more genres: poetry, fiction, personal essay, autobiography, screenwriting, drama, journalism, journal writing."

Director/Contact: Mary Beth O'Connor, Margo Gumosky, Kit Wainer, Co-Directors

Location(s): campus of Hobart-William Smith Colleges, Geneva, NY

Dates: Mid-July, 1996

Commenced: 1974

Recent faculty/lecturers: Dorothy Allison, Kwelismith, Grace Paley, Shay Youngblood, Lucille Clifton

Enrollment: 25-35; *Enrollment limit:* 35

Scholarships: yes—manuscript required

Ancillary activities: readings, panels, anthology

HOFSTRA UNIVERSITY SUMMER WRITERS' CONFERENCE
110 Hofstra University
Hempstead, New York 11550-1090
tel: (516) 463-5016
fax: (516) 463-4833

A ten-day conference "which offers a choice of five daily workshops led by master writers and includes individual conferences with these writers together with assorted presentations related to the writing process." Included are fiction, nonfiction, poetry, screenwriting, children's literature.

Director/Contact: Lewis Shena, Director

Location(s): Hofstra University, Hempstead, New York

Dates: 2nd week in July, 1996

Commenced: 1973

Recent faculty/lecturers: Lynne Tillman, Jan Marino, David Bouchier, Martine Bellen, Nilo Cruz

Manuscripts: required, if seeking credit; *Individual manuscript conferencing:* yes

Agents/editors attend: yes; *Available for conferencing:* yes

Enrollment: 60; *Enrollment limit:* 16 per workshop

Ancillary activities: readings and special speakers, tie-ins to a local folk and film festival

MANHATTANVILLE'S SUMMER WRITERS' WORKSHOP
2900 Purchase Street
Purchase, NY 10577
tel: (914) 694-3425
fax: (914) 694-3488

A five-day conference with "workshops offered in specific genres: fiction, short fiction, creative nonfiction, children's literature, poetry, personal essay, the writer's craft, script writing."

Director/Contact: Ruth Dowd, RSCJ, Dean, Adult and Special Programs

Locations: Manhattanville College, Purchase, NY

Dates: June 24-28, 1996

Commenced: 1983

Recent faculty/lecturers: Philip Lopate, Elizabeth Winthrop, Maureen Howard, Raphael Yglesias, Marita Golden, Lore Segal, Mark Doty

Manuscripts: required; *Individual manuscript conferencing:* yes; *Editing assistance:* yes; *Marketing guidance:* yes

Agents/editors attend: yes

Enrollment: 80-85; *Enrollment limit:* 15 per workshop, 7-8 workshops

Ancillary activities: readings by author/workshop leaders, special lecture by well-known author, session with editor and agent

NEW YORK STATE SUMMER WRITER'S INSTITUTE
Skidmore College
Saratoga Springs, NY 12866-1632
tel: (518) 584-5000, ext. 2264

Jointly sponsored by the Office of the Dean of Special Programs at Skidmore College and the University of Albany, this four-week program features "creative writing programs in fiction, nonfiction and poetry... Standard three-hour class meetings [workshops] three days each week will be supplemented by a program of Tuesday and Thursday afternoon roundtable sessions with visiting faculty." Both undergraduate and graduate credit opportunities are available.

Director/Contact: Robert Boyers, Director, Marc Woodworth, Assistant Director

Location(s): campus of Skidmore College, Saratoga Springs, NY

Dates: July 2-28, 1996

Commenced: 1987

Recent faculty/lecturers: Susan Sontag, William Kennedy, Joyce Carol Oates, Bharati Mukherjee, Robert Pinsky, Louise Gluck, Ann Beattie, Russell Banks, Marilynne Robinson, Michael Ondaatje, Oscar Hijuelos

Manuscripts: required; *Individual manuscript conferencing:* yes; *Editing assistance:* yes

Enrollment: 140; *Enrollment limit:* 16 per workshop

Scholarships: yes

Ancillary activities: nightly public readings by staff and visiting writers during the week; weekend publishing symposia and student readings

SOUTHAMPTON WRITERS' WORKSHOPS
Summer Office, Southampton College
239 Montauk Hwy
Southampton, NY 11968-4198
tel: (516) 287-8349 • *fax:* (516) 283-4081

Offering 4-5 workshops for one credit in the summer, covering "fiction, nonfiction, poetry, play writing, children's literature and others."

Director/Contact: Carla Caglioti, Summer Director

Location(s): Southampton College, eastern tip of Long Island, NY

Dates: July, 1996

Commenced: 1975

Recent faculty/lecturers: Robert Olen Butler, M.E. Kerr, Louis Simpson, Betty Freidan, Kurt Vonnegut

Individual manuscript conferencing: yes

Enrollment: 45; *Enrollment limit:* 15 per workshop

Ancillary activities: student and author readings, one-day writers' festival

WRITERS '96 WRITERS' CONFERENCE
National Writers Union
Westchester/Fairfield Local
P.O. Box 294
White Plains, NY 10602
tel: (914) 472-8438

Full one-day conference sponsored by the Westchester/Fairfield local of the National Writers Union with "seminars on a full range of topics from poetry and short fiction to travel writing and self promotion. Keynote speaker."

Director/Contact: Linda Simone, President

Location(s): Mercy College, Dobbs Ferry, NY

Dates: April, 1996

Commenced: 1984

Recent faculty/lecturers: Dana Givia, Izzy Gesell, Dan Wakefield, Mary Kaye Blakely, Susan Farewell, Arthur Herzog, Ann E. Dunne

Manuscript: required by some seminar leaders

Agents/editors attend: yes; *Available for conferencing:* yes

Scholarships: yes

Ancillary activities: poetry and fiction readings.

THE WRITER'S VOICE OF THE SILVER BAY ASSOCIATION
Route 9N
Silver Bay, NY 12874
tel: (518) 543-8833 • *fax:* (518) 543-6733

This is a YMCA conference center which "offers 3 to 4 workshops each spring; an eight week reading series, 'Readings by the Bay', in summer; two master-level residencies in summer and [a] focus on school residencies in the fall." Covered are fiction, nonfiction and poetry.

Director/Contact: Sharon, R. Ofner, Director

Location(s): Silver Bay Association, Silver Bay, NY

Dates: spring, summer and fall, 1996

Commenced: 1991

Recent faculty/lecturers: James Howard Kuntsler, Mark Nepo, Adrienne Rich, Jessica Hagedorn, Martin Espada, Susan Hubbard, Douglas Glover

Manuscripts: required for residencies only

Enrollment: 12 per workshop or residency

Ancillary activities: Silver Bay Children's Literature Award for best manuscript set in the Adirondack Mountains of New York; readings in July and August

NORTH CAROLINA

THE NORTH CAROLINA WRITERS' NETWORK
FALL CONFERENCE
P.O. Box 954
Carrboro, NC 27570
tel: (919) 967-9540
fax: (919) 929-0535

This conference "brings together writers, editors, agents and publishers for an intensive weekend of workshops, panel discussions, readings and entertainment." Areas covered include poetry, writing for children, fiction, nonfiction, essay. The conference is sponsored by a nonprofit literary organization with members throughout the state.

Director/Contact: Marsha Warren, Executive Director

Location (s): Triangle area (Raleigh, Durham, Chapel Hill, NC)

Dates: early-mid November, 1996

Commenced: 1984

Recent faculty/lecturers: Amos De Eavan Boland, Carolyn Forche, Roy Blount, Lee Smith, Robert Morgan, Gwendolyn Parker, Randall Kenan, Ed Sanders, John Ehle

Marketing guidance: yes

Agents/editors attend: yes; *Available for conferencing:* yes

Enrollment: 400 +; *Enrollment limit:* certain classes are available on a first-come, first-serve basis

Scholarships: yes, for both teachers and students; contact the Network in July or August prior to the conference

Ancillary activities: vendor/bookseller area, open-mike readings, NCWN annual meeting

NORTH DAKOTA

UNIVERSITY OF NORTH DAKOTA ANNUAL WRITERS' CONFERENCE

English Dept.
Box 7029
University Station
Grand Forks, ND 58202
tel: (701) 777-2864
fax: (701) 777-3650

A five-day reading conference where "5-6 writers participate in panel discussions and read from their works. No manuscript consultation is offered," and there are no workshops.

Director/Contact: Robert King, Director

Location(s): Memorial Union, University of North Dakota, Grand Forks, ND

Dates: mid-March, 1996

Commenced: 1970

Recent faculty/lecturers: Tim O'Brien, Yusef Komunyakaa, Sharon Olds, Sherman Alexie, Baharti Mukherjee, Jonis Agree, Sandra Benitez, Larry Watson, Ana Castillo

Agents/editors attend: infrequently

Enrollment: 200 at each session—no enrollment limit

Ancillary activities: all readings open to the public

OHIO

CEDAR HILLS CHRISTIAN WRITING WEEKEND
5811 Vrooman Road
Painesville, OH 44077
tel: (216) 352-6363

A weekend-long conference devoted to "fiction, nonfiction, poetry, articles, all with a Christian accent."

Director/Contact: Lea Leever Oldham, Coordinator

Location(s): Cedar Hills Conference Center, Painesville, OH

Dates: mid-June, 1996

Commenced: 1995

Recent faculty/lecturers: Lea Leever Oldham, Bob Grgic, Mary Ann Slattery

Individual manuscript conferencing: yes; *Editing assistance:* yes; *Marketing guidance:* yes

Enrollment: 70-80—no enrollment limit for day students

COLUMBUS WRITERS' CONFERENCE
P.O. Box 20548
Columbus, OH 43220
tel: (614) 451-0216 • *fax:* (614) 451-0174

A one-day conference covering long and short fiction, as well as genre fiction in mystery and science fiction, children's literature, humor, screen writing, television writing.

Director/Contact: Angela Palazzolo, Producer

Location(s): The Fawcett Center for Tomorrow, Columbus, OH

Dates: September, 1996

Commenced: 1993

Recent faculty/lecturers: Tracey E. Dils, Mike Harden, Les Roberts, Dennis McKiernan, Linda Taylor, Lee Abbott, Mary Ann Henry

Marketing guidance: yes—in group presentation

Agents/editor attend: yes

Enrollment: 200

Ancillary activities: book sale, book signings

THE HEIGHTS WRITERS' CONFERENCE
Writer's World Press
Cleveland, OH 44124
tel: (216) 481-1974 • *fax:* (216) 481-2057

A one-day program "for anyone interested in writing and publishing. It offers concurrent seminars in areas that will help beginners get started (manuscript preparation, query letters, book proposals etc.), genre writing and workshops for more established writers." Covered are fiction, historical romance, science fiction, mystery, children's literature, nonfiction, poetry.

Director/Contact: Lavern Hall, Conference Coordinator

Location(s): Cleveland, OH

Dates: May, 1996

Commenced: 1992

Recent faculty/lecturers: Les Roberts, Mary Grimm, June Lund Shiplett, Darlene Montonaro, Steve Grants, Patricia Fernberg, Eileen Beal, Lea Leever Oldham, Kate Kilbank

Individual manuscript conferencing: yes; *Editing assistance:* yes; *Marketing guidance:* yes

Agents/editors attend: yes; *Available for conferencing:* yes

Enrollment: 100-150; *Enrollment limit:* 25 in workshops

Ancillary activities: free handouts, local book shop sets up and offers writers' and small publishers' books, networking reception and author book signing

IMAGINATION
English Dept.
Cleveland State University
Cleveland, OH 44115
tel: (216) 687-4522
fax: (216) 687-6943

A five-day conference covering "fiction, poetry, science fiction. Morning workshops, afternoon lectures. Discussions, panels and readings." On Saturday there is a colloquium on the business of writing.

Director/Contact: Dr. Neal Chandler, Director of Creative Writing Program

Location(s): Mather Mansion, campus of Cleveland State University, Cleveland, OH

Dates: July 11-16, 1996

Commenced: 1991

Recent faculty/lecturers: Karen Joy Fowler, Rick Hillis, Reginald McKnight, Pat Murphy, Shiela Schwartz, Tim Seibles, John Nichols, Ruth Stone, Liz Rosenberg

Manuscript: required for workshops, not for conferences; *Individual manuscript conferencing:* yes; *Editing assistance:* yes; *Marketing guidance:* yes

Agents/editors attend: yes; *Available for conferencing:* yes

Enrollment: 80-90; *Enrollment limit:* 10 per workshop

Scholarships: yes, indicate need in note submitted with application

Ancillary activities: Poets League of Greater Cleveland contest and publication

MEET... NEAL CHANDLER

PROGRAM DIRECTOR, IMAGINATION

HOW DO YOU CHOOSE someone to run a writers' conference? Shouldn't it be a person who teaches English and who *understands*!

In 1988-89 Cleveland State University in Ohio wanted to start a writers' conference. There was Neal Chandler, the Director of the Creative Writing Program. A perfect fit, it seemed.

The only problem was that Neal Chandler had never run a writers' conference. In fact, he had taught German for fifteen years! "I came into this from pretty far away," he admits, but he's a resourceful man, and he had a major asset to call upon.

"When I started the creative writing program,"` he says, "one of the first people we brought in was Karen Fowler, a science fiction writer, whose work we liked." Fowler, who had appeared at numerous writers' conferences, taught a public, no-credit, fiction workshop at Cleveland State University that was popular and successful, and she was an excellent teacher. By transcending science fiction and encouraging all forms of fiction, she had students respecting each other's work within two weeks. "What she wouldn't let them do was fight the genre fights. She talked about writing generally, was it good, was it successful, was it strong or not strong?"

So Neal Chandler spoke with Karen Fowler. "The first thing we agreed upon was the issue of genre. It wasn't something we wanted to bracket out." he says, "we were willing to invite people who did so-called genre work as well as those who didn't. What we wanted was to invite people who did strong writing, *period*!"

And that's been the hallmark of the program. From the beginning Karen Fowler has been Chair of the Conference Faculty, and Neal Chandler has been Director of the Program. "That means," says Chandler, "she looks after the faculty while I manage schedules, contracts, budgets, publicity and paper cups." Or, as Chandler ruefully admits, Fowler represents labor while he represents management.

An early innovation was to make it possible so every student could work with each workshop leader. There are six workshops (usually four fiction workshops and two poetry workshops) and the students are broken into groups of ten. "Students often complain they come to a conference because they'll be able to work with some special writer, and then they find the workshop filled." But not at this conference. "As we cycle workshop groups through, every day the leader changes, and we find the students love this approach. In the afternoons I ask each workshop leader to take over a lecture or a discussion group, and you get a whole range of material here."

Chandler calls his conference "manuscript intensive." Students must submit a manuscript well ahead of the conference, and these are circulated to the group leaders and each member of the workshop at least two weeks before the conference begins. "Everyone in the seminar has read the manuscript before they walk through the door, and, in addition, each student has an individual conference with a second leader." Chandler laughs. "You should see my mailing and xeroxing budget. It's a hell of a lot of work to get all these manuscripts out to everyone."

About eighty percent of those who apply to this writers' conference get accepted, and many of them come from Ohio and are not affluent. But Chandler's expectations don't vary regardless of economic or geographic state. "I want two things in the people who apply to this conference," he says. "First, I want to be sure they're already working at a level where they're comfortable so they don't feel like they're in foreign straits. Second, I want people here who really want to be in the workshops, not those who may have some other agenda."

He's an optimistic man, is Neal Chandler. "If we get someone who shows promise, we take them, we don't wait," he says. "What we want students to do at the workshops is to learn something."

MIDWEST WRITERS' CONFERENCE

Kent State University, Stark Campus
6000 Frank Avenue N.W.
Canton, OH 44720
tel: (216) 499-9600
fax: (216) 494-6121

A two-day conference "open to writers in any category to provide an atmosphere in which aspiring writers can meet with and learn from experienced, established writers through lectures, workshops, contests, personal interviews and informal group discussions." Covered are fiction, nonfiction, poetry and children's literature.

Director/Contact: Gregg L. Andrews, Director, Special Programs and Continuing Studies

Location(s): Stark Campus of Kent State University, Canton, OH

Dates: October 4-5, 1996

Commenced: 1968

Recent faculty/lecturers: keynoters have included Joyce Carol Oates, John Updike, Kurt Vonnegut, Edward Albee

Individual manuscript conferencing: yes; *Marketing guidance:* yes

Agents/editors attend: yes; *Available for conferencing:* yes

Enrollment: 350—no enrollment limit

Scholarships: student discounts are available

Ancillary activities: readings and book fair; competitive writing contests and critiques in fiction, nonfiction, poetry and children's literature

READING, WRITING AND ROMANCE CONFERENCE
OV Romance Writers Association
72 Cherokee Drive
Hamilton, OH 45013-4910
tel: (513) 863-6053

One-day conference specializing in romance-genre fiction for levels of ability.

Director/Contact: Linda Keller, President

Location(s): vary from year to year

Dates: 2nd Saturday, February, 1996

Commenced: 1991

Individual manuscript conferencing: yes; *Editing assistance:* yes; *Marketing guidance:* yes

Agents/editors attend: yes; *Available for conferencing:* yes

Enrollment: 200; *Enrollment limit:* 300

Ancillary activities: book-signing party, fiction contest

WESTERN RESERVE WRITERS & FREELANCE CONFERENCE
WESTERN RESERVE WRITERS' MINI CONFERENCE
34200 Ridge Rd #110
Willoughby, OH 44094
tel: (216) 943-3047 • (800) OLDHAM 1

One-day conferences covering as follows: Writers and Freelance: fiction (short story and novel), poetry, science fiction, romance, mystery writing, screenwriting, articles, nonfiction books, tax and accounting information, copyright, marketing; Mini: fiction (short story and novel), science fiction, poetry, articles, nonfiction books, marketing.

Director/Contact: Lea Leever Oldham, Coordinator

Location(s): Lakeland Community College, Mentor, OH

Dates: Writers & Freelance: September 9, 1996
Mini: March 25, 1996

Commenced: Writers & Freelance: 1982
Mini: 1991

Recent faculty/lecturers: Les Roberts, Nina Coombs Pykare, Barbara Driemiller, Gail Bellamy, Mary Grimm, William Donahue Ellis, Eli Beachy

Individual manuscript conferencing: yes; *Marketing guidance:* yes

Agents/editors attend: sometimes

Enrollment: Writers & Freelance: 150; Mini: 125—no enrollment limit for either conference

Scholarships: yes, write for information

WRITING FOR MONEY
34200 Ridge Road, #110
Willoughby, OH 44094
tel: (216) 943-3047
(800) OLDHAM 1

One-day workshop covering "query letters, marketing, characterization, book proposals, multiple use of ideas, grammar, editing."

Director/Contact: Lee Leaver Oldham, teacher

Location(s): Mentor, Mayfield, Bedford, Madision, Cleveland Heights, OH

Dates: offered 3 or 4 times throughout 1996 at each location

Commenced: 1980

Recent faculty/lecturers: Lea Leever Oldham

Individual manuscript conferencing: yes; *Editing assistance:* yes; *Marketing guidance:* yes

Enrollment: varies

OKLAHOMA

NIMROD/OKLAHOMA WRITERS SYMPOSIUM

2210 South Main
Tulsa, OK 74114
tel: (918) 584-3333
fax: (918) 582-2787

A two-day symposium and workshop sponsored by the Arts and Humanities Council of Tulsa and NIMROD Magazine to honor the winners and judges of yearly fiction and poetry competitions. There "panel discussions by established writers on the writing process" and fiction and poetry workshops.

Director/Contact: Cheryl Gravis, Program Specialist: Literary Arts & Humanities & Managing Editor, NIMROD

Location(s): Tulsa, OK

Dates: October 18-19, 1996

Commenced: 1980

Recent faculty/lecturers: John Leonard, Toby Olson, Gladys Swan, Olga Broumas, James Ragan, W.D. Snodgrass

Manuscript: required for workshops

Agents/editors attend: yes

Enrollment: 75

Ancillary activities: readings, contests

OKLAHOMA FALL ARTS INSTITUTES
P.O. Box 18154
Oklahoma City, OK 73154
tel: (405) 842-0890
fax: (405) 848-4538

Weekend-long conference with workshops covering fiction, nonfiction, poetry, the Art of Teaching Writing and writing for children.

Director/Contact: Linda DeBerry, Assistant Program Director

Location(s): Quartz Mountain Arts and Conference Center, Lonewolf, OK

Dates: October, 1996

Commenced: 1983

Recent faculty/lecturers: Gail E. Haley, Leonard Tourney, Lee Gutkind, Olga Broumas, Reginald Gibbons

Enrollment: 100; *Enrollment limit:* 20 per class

Scholarships: yes, for Oklahoma residents

Ancillary activities: faculty presentations/readings, chamber music concert

OREGON

FISHTRAP
P.O. Box 38
Enterprise, OR 97828
tel: (503) 426-3623

This conference includes workshops and "gatherings" in summer and winter focusing on issues of writing and public policy and working in an intimate setting. Summer Fishtrap is a series of writing workshops (covering four days) on fiction, nonfiction, poetry, photography dealing with the American West. Immediately following the summer workshops is a weekend "gathering" with readings and roundtable discussion on writing and public policy; winter Fishtrap offers a fiction writing workshop as part of a weekend "gathering" that focuses natural resource issues and the writing about them.

Director/Contact: Rich Wandschneider, Director

Location (s): Wallowa Lake Camp, Wallowa, OR

Dates: Summer Fishtrap—early-mid July, 1996

Winter Fishtrap—mid-late February, 1996

Commenced: Summer Fishtrap—1987

Winter Fishtrap—1992

Recent faculty/lecturers: Summer—Ivan Doig, Kim Stafford, Jeanne Wakatsuke Houston, Alvin Josephy, Valerie Miner, Sandra Scofield; Winter—John Rember, Emily Swanson, Patricia McConnel, Mikal Gilmore, Richard Brown

Agents/editors attend: yes

Enrollment: 75 for the summer writing workshops; 100 for the summer "gathering"; 50 for the winter "gathering"; *Enrollment limit:* summer writing workshops limited to 12 per workshop, winter "gathering" limited to 50 attendees

Scholarships: yes, five fellowships awarded each year for Summer Fishtrap (submit a brief biography and a writing sample); six scholarships awarded each year, two through the Northwest Native American Writers, two through Northwest African-American writers' groups; two for high school or college students (submit a writing sample, a brief statement explaining financial need, a personal reference).

Ancillary activities: Summer Fishtrap—readings, panel discussion, open mike, organized hikes, barbeque; Winter Fishtrap—swim, moonlight ski, readings, open mike, book signings

MEET...
RICH WANDSCHNEIDER

DIRECTOR, FISHTRAP, INC.

"IT SORT OF HAPPENED without anyone planning it," says Rich Wandschneider, referring to Fishtrap, Inc. where he is director and unofficial historian. "Back in 1986, a couple of people wanted to to organize a northwest writers' group, but they were all on the Oregon coast." Wandschneider lived and worked in northeastern Oregon, operated a bookstore there and wanted awareness his locale was special and distinctive. "It's Nez Perce Country," he says, and he didn't want that connection buried.

It was suggested he organize a writers' gathering in eastern Oregon. He had no plan, but he did have a friend, Alvin Josephy, who lived nearby and who had been a war correspondent and editor of *Time* and *American Heritage*. When Wandschneider mentioned the idea, Josephy filled with enthusiasm. "He said, 'I've got these guys in New York I'd love to get out here. They send me books to review about the West, but they don't even know the right books to send.'" Wandschneider and Josephy talked some more; Josephy contacted his New York agent, Julian Bach, editor Marc Jaffe with Houghton-Mifflin and Naomi Bliven from *The New Yorker*, and they agreed to come. Wandschneider contacted several western writers, including Craig Leslie and Ursula Le Guin. Suddenly, they had a writers' conference... and a ready-made theme: Western Writing, Eastern Publishing.

The next year came the idea that workshops ought to be part of the conference. "We thought," says Wandschnieder, "these people [the faculty] are coming, they're here, let's do a workshop." But with limits: these would be writing workshops, not manuscript workshops. "I'd rather have people write here, not go over old manuscripts; we don't jury people in; it's been our policy right along: no manuscript review."

Since its first year, Fishtrap has been held at Wallowa Lake Camp in the top right-hand corner of Oregon. The accomodations are rustic but comfortable, with swimming, boating, camping and horses to ride. And things have grown, indeed! Now, there's the summer writers' conference on a chosen theme that runs for four days in early July, followed immediately by "the gathering," which carries through the weekend and is attended by many who haven't come to the writers' conference. The Fishtrap "gathering" adds librarians, booksellers, teachers to a coterie of writers' conference attendees who have stayed on. Here the emphasis is on readings and discussions of the theme or themes that underlay the just-concluded writers' conference.

Then, six months later, there's Winter Fishtrap, a workshop/gathering at the same location. It's limited to fifty people and offers four presenters, and it's *not* a writers' conference. "We get into policy issues, not writing issues," says Wandschneider. "We mix up historians, fiction writers, journalists, public officials and professionals."

In the summer about seventy five people attend the writers' conference. "Eight to ten writers come, and we limit the workshops to twelve people," Wandschneider says. The workshops meet three hours a day for four days, and in the evening there are readings and open-mike opportunities. "What's innovative about our program is the idea there are no stars; we're not built around one or two people; also, we do themes, and we're not stuck on genres. So we put journalists together with poets, fiction writers together with biographers. You don't have poets talking to poets, historians talking to historians."

Along with the writing, Fishtrap teaches *reading*, that is, how to read what you've written to an audience. "We have open mikes every night, and the students are encouraged to participate. Workshop instructors often take a few moments and say, 'Let's talk about selecting what you're going to read, let's talk about pace, about crowding too much into your time.' It seems to work well."

How about that name, Fishtrap? "Our conferences are held in the Wallowa Mountains of eastern Oregon," says Wandschneider, "in Wallowa County, on Wallowa Lake." Remember the Nez Perce connection and Rich Wandschneider's desire to preserve it? " 'Wallowa' is a Nez Perce word that refers to the anchors of fishtraps the Indians used to trap the big river salmon. It fits, we think."

HAYSTACK WRITING PROGRAM
Portland State University
School of Extended Studies
P.O. Box 1491
Portland, OR 97207
tel: (800) 547-8887 • *fax:* (503) 725-4840

"One-week intensive writing workshops in fiction, nonfiction, memoir, mystery, playwriting, screenwriting, poetry, chldren's literature."

Director/Contact: Maggie Herrington

Location (s): Cannon Beach, OR (north Oregon coast)

Dates: late June-early July, 1996

Commenced: 1968

Recent faculty/lecturers: Molly Gloss, Tom Spanbauer, Mark Medoff, Sandra McPherson, Sallie Tisdale, Craig Lesley

Editing assistance: yes; *Marketing guidance:* yes

Enrollment: 150; *Enrollment limit:* 15 per workshop

Ancillary activities: author readings, beach gatherings

ROGUE VALLEY WRITERS' CONFERENCE
Continuing Education
Southern Oregon State College
Ashland, OR 97520
tel: (903) 552-6901 • *fax:* (903) 652-6047

A five-day conference featuring "full morning workshops on fiction, nonfiction, poetry, science fiction, dramatic writing, freelance writing, family history. Concurrent afternoon workshops on a wide variety of relevant topics. Prominent keynote speaker and guest lecturers."

Director/Contact: Celeste Stevens, Special Programs Coordinator

Location (s): campus of Southern Oregon State College, Ashland, OR

Dates: July 8-12, 1996

Commenced: 1989

Recent faculty/lecturers: Jean Auel, Lawson Inada, Sandra Scofield, Kenn Goddard, Linda Eckhardt, P.K. Hallinan

Manuscripts: required; *Individual manuscript conferencing:* yes; *Editing assistance:* yes; *Marketing guidance:* yes

Agents/editors attend: editors only

Enrollment: 80; *Enrollment limit:* 85-90

Ancillary activities: readings

THE ARTS AT MENUCHA
P.O. Box 4958
Portland, OR 97208
tel: (503) 760-5837

Two five-day workshops, one in poetry, one in fiction taught by well-known writers, "but instructors are usually willing to help with all kinds of writing." Sponsored by the Creative Arts Community of Menucha at an old country estate of one of Oregon's former governors that overlooks the Columbia River.

Director/Contact: John Kinyou, Ass't to the President

Location: Menucha, OR

Dates: second and third weeks, August, 1996

Commenced: 1965

Recent faculty/lecturers: Patricia Goedicke, Lucille Clifton, Naomi Shihab Nye, William Strafford, Lisa Steinman, Doug Marx, Margaret Chula

Individual manuscript conferencing: yes; *Editing assistance:* yes

Enrollment: 10 per workshop

Scholarships: yes

Ancillary activities: readings

THE FLIGHT OF THE MIND,
SUMMER WRITING WORKSHOPS FOR WOMEN
622 S.E. 29th Avenue
Portland, OR 97214
tel: (503) 236-9862

"Two separate week-long residential workshops. Each week has five classes including fiction, poetry, nonfiction, play writing, children's literature and special topics."

Director/Contact: Judith Barrington, Director

Dates: June 14-21, June 23-30, 1996

Commenced: 1984

*Recent faculty/lecturers:*Ursula K. LeGuin, Grace Paley, Evelyn C. White, Naomi Shinar Nye, Elizabeth Woody, Barbara Wilson, Janile Gould, Judith Barrington

Manuscript: required; *Marketing guidance:* yes

Agents/editors attend: editors only; *Available for conferencing:* yes, in group session

Enrollment: 65 per week; *Enrollment limit:* 14 per class

Scholarships: yes, for a variety of categories

Ancillary activities: evening programs, faculty and participant readings, peer critique groups

PENNSYLVANIA

BUCKNELL SEMINAR FOR YOUNGER POETS

Stadler Center for Poetry
Bucknell University
Lewisburg, PA 17837
tel: (717) 524-1853
fax: (717) 524-3760

"Ten undergraduates from American colleges spend four weeks writing poetry, attending workshops, reading from their work. Staff is available for tutorials."

Location(s): campus of Bucknell University, Lewisburg, PA

Dates: mid-June to mid-July, 1996

Commenced: 1985

Recent faculty/lecturers: John Wheatcroft, Karl Patten, Deirdre O'Connor, Steven Styers, Bruce Smith, Gerald Stern, Molly Peacock, Collete Inez

Manuscripts: required; *Individual manuscript conferencing:* yes; *Editing assistance:* yes; *Marketing guidance:* yes

Enrollment: 10; *Enrollment limit:* 10

Scholarships: yes; Bucknell provides tuition, board, room and spaces for writing

Ancillary activities: poetry readings, watching videos on poets and poetry, lectures on editing and publishing and translating poetry; chapbook published containing work of students

CUMBERLAND VALLEY FICTION WRITERS' WORKSHOP

Dickinson College
P.O. Box 1773
Carlisle, PA 17013-2896
tel: (717) 245-1291
fax: (717) 245-1942

A six-day workshop concentrating on fiction writing only with classes, readings and panel discussions.

Director/Contact: Judy Gill, Director

Location(s): campus of Dickinson College, Carlisle, PA

Dates: June 23-28, 1996

Commenced: 1990

Recent faculty/lecturers: Lee K. Abbott, Madison Smartt Bell, Lorrie Moore, Robert Olmstead, Melissa Pritchard, Leigh Allison Wilson, Liza Wieland

Manuscript: required; *Individual manuscript conferencing:* yes; *Editing assistance:* yes; *Marketing guidance:* yes

Enrollment: 30-40; *Enrollment limit:* 40 (4 classes, ten per class)

Ancillary activities: nightly readings by faculty, roundtable discussions

OUTDOOR WRITERS ASSOCIATION OF AMERICA ANNUAL CONFERENCE

2017 Cato Avenue
State College, PA 16801-2768
tel: (814) 234-1011
fax: (814) 234-9692

A five-day conference devoted to "craft improvement seminars [in] radio, television, video, photography, writing, outdoor comunications." Sponsored by a "nonprofit, professional organization representing professional communicators who report and reflect upon America's diverse interest in the outdoors."

Director/Contact: James Rainey, Executive Director; Eileen King, Meeting Planner

Location(s): changes each year, Duluth, MN in 1996

Dates: June 16-20, 1996

Commenced: 1927

Recent facilty/lecturers: Bruce Babbitt, Petr Jacobi, Jeffrey Lant, Mollie Beattie, Dr Charles Graves, Norville Prosser, Stephan Rafe, Mike Hayden

Agents/editors attend: yes; *Available for conferencing:* yes

Enrollment: 900; *Enrollment limit:* must either be a member of OWAA or have prior approval from the executive director

Scholarships: yes—must be attending an OWAA-approved university/college (list is available at above address)

Ancillary activities: contests (for members only) in writing, photography, broadcast

PENNWRITERS CONFERENCE
RR 2, Box 241
Middlebury Center, PA 16935
tel: (717) 376-2821/3361 • *fax:* (717) 376-2674

Three-day conference for all levels of writing with workshops and roundtables on craft and techniques of mystery, horror and suspense writing, juvenile and young adult writing, and general fiction, nonfiction and screenwriting.

Director/Contact: C.J. Houghtaling, Coordinator

Location(s): Grantville Holiday Inn, Grantville, PA (near Hershey)

Dates: May 17-19, 1996

Commenced: 1989

Recent faculty/lecturers: Gary Provost, Molly Cochran, Michael Seidman, Julia Eklar, Warren Murphy, David K. Hartford

Marketing guidance: yes

Agents/editors attend: yes; *Available for conferencing:* yes

Enrollment: 150-200; *Enrollment limit:* 200

Ancillary activities: author's tea and autographing, "In Other Words" contest open to conference attendees in fiction, nonfiction, poetry

PITTSBURGH THEOLOGICAL SEMINARY WRITERS' WORKSHOP

616 North Highland Avenue
Pittsburgh, PA 15206
tel: (412) 362-5610
fax: (412) 363-3260

A two-to three-day conference that "covers all aspects of becoming published" including the preparation of manuscripts, obtaining editor interest, contracts and royalty agreements and the responsibilities for both author and editor.

Director/Contact: Rev. Mary Lee Talbot, Director of Continuing Education

Location(s): campus of Pittsburgh Theological Seminary, Pittsburgh, PA

Dates: late April-early May, 1996

Commenced: 1983

Recent faculty/lecturers: Dr. Roland Tapp

Individual manuscript conferencing: yes; *Editing assistance:* yes; *Marketing guidance:* yes

Enrollment: 25

WRITING FOR PUBLICATION SUCCESFULLY
Villanova University
Villanova, PA 19085
tel: (610) 519-4618
fax: (610) 519-4623

A two-day conference (which may be taken for graduate credit) "to encourage participants to consider personal and/or professional growth through writing for publication (journal, newspaper, magazine articles, books, etc.)" and "to provide participants with the knowledge, skills and attitudes necessary to successfully submit a manuscript for publication."

Director/Contact: Ray Heitzmann, Ph.D., Director

Location(s): campus of Villanova Univerisity, Villanova, PA

Dates: mid-late March, 1996

Commenced: 1975

Recent faculty/lecturers: Ray Heitzmann, Ph.D., Anthony D'Allessandro, Jean McWilliams, Edward Stranix

Individual manuscript conferencing: yes

Agents/editors attend: usually not, but if they do come, they will be available for conferencing

Enrollment: 20; ***Enrollment limit:*** 20 (in seminar format)

Ancillary activities: brown bag working lunch

RHODE ISLAND

COMMUNITY WRITERS' ASSOCIATION WRITING PROGRAM

Newport Writers' Conference
P.O. Box 12
Newport, RI 02840-0001
tel: (401) 846-9884
fax: (401) 683-6496

Program: "Six-week writing workshops held one evening per week." Covered are script writing, travel writing, journal writing, songwriting, beginning poetry, beginning and advanced fiction, writing for children, biography, feature writing.

Conference: small and intimate weekend with "workshops in fiction, magazine writing, screenwriting and writing for children." There is also a getting-published panel discussion.

Director/Contact: Eleyne Austen Sharp, Executive Director (both Program and Conference)

Location (s): Finnegan's Inn at Shadow Lawn, Middletown, RI and additional sites throughout Newport and Providence, RI

Dates: Program: January, March, May, July, September, November, 1996. Conference: mid-October, 1996

Commenced: 1995 (Program); 1992 (Conference)

Recent faculty/lecturers: Program: Tony Amore, Susan Grant, Karen Marlow. Conference: Gloria Nagy, Patricia Riley, Joan Millman, Tony Amore

Individual manuscript conferencing: yes (both); *Editing assistance:* yes (both); *Marketing guidance:* yes (both)

Agents/editors attend: yes, Conference only; *Available for conferencing:* yes, Conference only

Enrollment: 10 per workshop (both)

Scholarships: yes (both)

Ancillary activities: Program: annual CWA writing competition, open readings, instructional videotapes, CWA collaborative books, quarterly newsletter

SOUTH CAROLINA

CHARLESTON WRITERS' CONFERENCE

English Department
College of Charleston
Charleston, SC 29412
tel: (803) 953-5664
fax: (803) 953-3180

A multi-day conference that covers "readings, workshops, seminars, panels. Genres include fiction, nonfiction, poetry, play writing, screenwriting, writing for children, avant garde poetry and fiction, storytelling."

Director/Contact: Paul Allen, Director

Location(s): campus of College of Charleston, Charleston, SC

Dates: March, 1996

Commenced: 1988

Recent faculty/lecturers: Yusef Komunyakaa, Kelley Cherry, Bret Lott, Pattiann Rogers, John Frederick Nims, Marvin Bell, Paul Hoover, Rosellen Brown, Joy Williams

Individual manuscript conferencing: yes; *Editing assistance:* yes; *Marketing guidance:* yes

Agents/editors attend: yes; *Available for conferencing:* yes

Enrollment: 160; *Enrollment limit:* only on individual manuscript critiques

Ancillary activities: open mike readings at area coffeehouses, Faculty Choice Awards, parties

WRITE TO SELL: THE SOUTHEAST'S NUTS AND BOLTS WRITERS' CONFERENCE

782 Wofford Street
Rock Hill, SC 29730
tel: (803) 366-5440
fax: (803) 327-0692

A practical two-day conference with a number of workshops covering fiction and nonfiction and pointed to getting work published.

Director/Contact: Ron Chepesiuk, Director

Location(s): Rock Hill, SC

Dates: February, 1996

Commenced: 1991

Recent faculty/lecturers: Gary Provost, Susan Crawford, John Clausen

Individual manuscript conferencing: yes

Agents/editors attend: yes; *Available for conferencing;* yes

Enrollment: 100

TENNESSEE

SEWANEE WRITERS' CONFERENCE
310 St. Luke's Hall
735 University Avenue
Sewanee, TN 37383-1000
tel: (615) 598-1141 • *fax:* (615) 598-1145

"Backed by the Walter E. Dakin Memorial Fund established through the estate of the late Tennessee Williams, the Conference will gather a distinguished faculty to provide instruction & criticism through workshops and craft lectures in fiction, poetry and play writing. In addition, each participant meets individually with a faculty member to discuss the member's manuscript."

Director/Contact: Wyatt Prunty, Director; Cheri Peters, Conference Administrator

Location(s): campus of the University of the South, Sewanee, TN

Dates: last two weeks, July, 1996

Commenced: 1990

Recent faculty/lecturers: Russell Banks, James Gordon Bennett, John Casey, Ellen Douglas, Ann Hood, Alice McDermott, Francine Prose, Stephen Wright, Anthony Hecht, John Hollander, Charles Martin, Mary Jo Salter, Kent Brown, Horton Foote

Manuscripts: required; *Individual manuscript conferencing:* yes; *Editing assistance:* yes; *Marketing guidance:* yes

Agents/editors attend: yes; *Available for conferencing:* some agents require recommendation from faculty members, others do not

Enrollment: 105; *Enrollment limit:* 15 per workshop

Scholarships: yes—additional forms required

Ancillary activities: guest, faculty and fellow readings; open mike readings for other participants

MEET... WYATT PRUNTY

Director, Sewanee Writers' Conference

W HAT'S IT LIKE to shoulder a literary gift from one of the century's most esteemed writers? Ask Wyatt Prunty, and he'll say it's exciting and rewarding... and a major opportunity to pass on the gift to others.

In 1988 Prunty, a tall, courtly man, was teaching in the MFA program at Johns Hopkins University in Baltimore when he received a call from Sewanee (known as the University of the South) in Tennessee. "They said they were looking for a writer- in- residence and was I interested," he recalls. Years before he had spent a semester writing at Sewanee as a Brown Foundation fellow. "I knew Sewanee had a long history of writers passing through and living there, but it had been mostly informal, though some would stay for awhile and edit *The Sewanee Review*." Still, there was rich literary tradition, and Prunty can recite names from the 1940s, 50s and 60s: Alan Tate, Monroe Spears, Caroline Gordon, Peter Taylor, Eleanor Ross Taylor, Robert Penn Warren, Ford Madox Ford, Jean Stafford, Robert Lowell. "These people would join forces, they'd drink and do charades and read to one another what they had been working on, so that in an informal way there was a literary community."

Prunty signed on in 1989, aware that Sewanee's rich literary tradition was about to expand. Tennessee Williams, one of America's foremost playwrights, had left a major sum of money to Sewanee, and the idea was to start a writer's conference. "Williams was very generous," Prunty says, "he was in the habit of giving money away, and when he died he had a million dollars in his checking account. When he learned someone was down and out, and he thought they had ability, he used to send them money."

But throughout his life Tennessee Williams never laid eyes on Sewanee. So why here? He had a grandfather, Walter E. Dakin, an Episcopal priest, who had gone to Sewanee and had returned every summer for vacations. "Walter Dakin was the one major stable male figure in Williams' life," Prunty says, "and he had great faith in the integrity of Sewanee based upon his grandfather's opinion of the place." So Tennessee Williams left money to Sewanee in his grandfather's name, remembering "all those stories from his grandfather about the wonderful artists and writers who passed through."

The first Sewanee Writers' Conference took place in 1990, and there were 72 open slots and three times as many applicants. In following years the number of slots has remained the same, but, as Prunty says, "the number of people applying has gone up dramatically, and so we have become quite selective." Manuscripts are required, and copies are sent to faculty prior to the opening of the conference. "So there's a body of material already in place that's going to be discussed."

He's particularly pleased with the faculty he's been able to attract: Derek Wolcott, Mona Van Dyne, Howard Nemerov, Donald Justice, William Styron, Arthur Miller, Horton Foote, among others. While he doesn't change the faculty totally each year, he does rotate them, and he's limited the conference workshops to fiction, poetry and play writing. "We don't do nonfiction prose at this point," he admits, "though there's a lot to be said for it, there's a pretty good demand for it and it's marketable. But," he adds, "we do bring in the very best editors and agents, and both large and small presses."

Prunty is pleased with the way his conference has grown and with how the literary gift from Tennessee Williams has been assimilated. "What distinguishes our writers' conference from others," he says, "is the quality of the student work and the reputation of the faculty. Whatever faculty you select, that's going to determine to a certain extent who applies to your program. If there's anything that can be said about a workshop, it's that the more talented students you have, the more dynamic, the more exciting the workshop is going to be."

WRITERS' WORKSHOP
Baptist Sunday School Board
P.O. Box 24001
Nashville, TN 37202
tel: (615) 251-2294

A five-day conference with a "focus on curriculum, articles, devotional and book writing. Major presentations by outside specialists, and conferences with key editors and published writers."

Director/Contact: Dr. Michael Fink, Workshop Coordinator

Location(s): Church Program Training Center, North Nashville, TN

Dates: July 15-19, 1996

Commenced: 1973-4

Recent faculty/lecturers: Robert Hastings, Carolyn Tomlin

Editing assistance: yes; *Marketing guidance:* yes

Enrollment: 55-60; *Enrollment limit:* 70

TEXAS

AMERICAN CHRISTIAN WRITERS CONFERENCE
(held January, 1996 in Houston, TX;
held May, 1996 in Dallas, TX. See Arizona for details)

ANNUAL WRITER'S CONFERENCE
Northeast Texas Writer's Organization
P.O. Box 675
Mt. Pleasant, TX 75456-0675
tel: (903) 537-4292

"A one-day conference that focuses primarily on fiction and nonfiction" and offers speakers throughout the day. The conference is co-sponsored by the Northeast Texas Writer's Organization and Northeast Texas Community College.

Director/Contact: Jean Pamplin, Program Chair, Northeast Texas Writer's Organization; Dr. Charlotte Biggerstaff, Dean of Continuing Education, Northeast Texas Community College

Location(s): campus of Northeast Texas Community College, Mt. Pleasant, TX

Dates: April, 1996

Commenced: 1986

Recent faculty/lecturers: Frank Vick, Zinita Fowler, C.J. Wright, John McCord

Editing assistance: yes; *Marketing guidance:* yes

Agents/editors attend: yes; *Available for conferencing:* yes

Scholarships: yes

CRAFT OF WRITING CONFERENCE
University of Texas at Dallas Center for Continuing Education
P.O. Box 830688
CN1.1
Richardson, TX 75083-0688
tel: (214) 883-2204
fax: (214) 883-2995

"This two-day conference for beginning to experienced writers offers workshops on a variety of topics, manuscript critique clinics and a manuscript awards contest." Covered are fiction, nonfiction, poetry, children's literature, play writing, screenwriting.

Director/Contact: Janet Harris, Director, Center for Continuing Education, University of Texas at Dallas

Location(s): Dallas, TX area

Dates: September, 1996

Commenced: 1982

Recent faculty/lecturers: Millard Lampell, Jerry Gross, C. Dean Anderson, Patricia Anthony, Claire Bocardo, Robert Flynn, Debbie Dadey, Laura Castoro, Francis Ray

Editing assistance: yes; *Marketing guidance:* yes

Agents/editors attend: yes; *Available for conferencing:* yes

Enrollment: 175—no enrollment limit

Ancillary activities: book sale and autography session, manuscript awards contest, banquet

GOLDEN TRIANGLE WRITER'S GUILD CONFERENCE
4245 Calder Avenue
Beaumont, TX 77705
tel: (409) 898-4894

A Thursday-Sunday conference with numerous workshops on a variety of genres, including fiction, nonfiction, mystery, romance, western, horror, script writing. The conference is sponsored by Golden Triangle Writer's Guild, a writer's support group.

Director/Contact: Rebecca Blanchard, Administrative Assistant

Location (s): Holiday Inn, Beaumont, TX

Dates: 2nd weekend in October, 1996

Commenced: 1984

Recent faculty: Ridley Pearson, Andrew Neiderman, Nora Roberts, Robert Vaughn, William Johnstone, Emma Merritt

Agents/editors attend: yes; *Available for conferencing:* yes

Enrollment: 400

Scholarships: yes—a limited number

Ancillary activities: unpublished writers contest

North Central Texas Chapter, SCBWI
1904 Tameria Drive
Irving TX 75060
tel: (214) 251-1013

A one-day conference for fiction writers and illustrators of children's literature, sponsored by the North Central Texas Chapter of the Society of Children's Book Writers and Illustrators.

Director/Contact: Crosby G. Holden

Location(s): Haggar Center, University of Dallas, Irving, TX

Dates: September, 1996

Commenced: 1983

Recent faculty/lecturers: Kathryn Hewitt, Gary Clifton Wisler, Harriet Barton, Elizabeth Law

Agents/editors attend: yes

Enrollment: 120; *Enrollment limit:* 150

RICE UNIVERSITY WRITERS' CONFERENCE
School of Continuing Studies
Rice University
6100 Main Street, Mail Stop 550
Houston, TX 77005-1892
tel: (713) 527-4803
fax: (713) 285-5213

Two-day conference with workshops in fiction, children's literature, poetry, screenplays, play writing.

Director/Contact: School of Continuing Studies

Location(s): campus of Rice University, Houston, TX

Dates: June 7-8, 1996

Commenced: 1992

Manuscripts: optional; *Individual manuscript conferencing:* optional

Agents/editors attend: yes; *Available for conferencing:* yes, in small groups

Ancillary activities: critique corners, manuscript contest, autograph party

ROMANCE WRITERS OF AMERICA ANNUAL CONFERENCE

13700 Veterans Memorial Drive
Suite #315
Houston, TX 77014
tel: (713) 440-6885
fax: (713) 440-7510

A five-day conference with more than 90 workshops and panels, guest speakers, appointments with agents, editors and an awards banquet.

Director/Contact: Linda Fisher, Executive Manager

Location(s): Loew's Anatole Hotel, Dallas, TX

Dates: July 10-14, 1996

Commenced: 1981

Recent faculty/lecturers: Nora Roberts, Linda Lael Miller, Sandra Brown, Sandra Canfield

Agents/editors attend: yes; *Available for conferencing:* yes

Enrollment: 2000—no enrollment limit, conference and workshops are open to all RWA members

Ancillary activities: annual contests: Golden Heart and RITA awards; Bi-monthly magazine—Romance Writers' Report

UTAH

Southern Utah Creative Writing Conference

Southern Utah University
Cedar City, UT 84720
tel: (801) 586-7839
(801) 586-1995

A one-week conference with workshops in fiction, nonfiction, poetry, play writing.

Director/Contact: David Lee, Dept. of Language and Literature; David Nyman, Continuing Education

Location(s): Mountain Learning Center, Southern Utah University, Cedar City, UT

Dates: July 14-19, 1996

Commenced: 1973

Recent faculty/lecturers: Bill Holm, William Stafford, Marvin Bell, Terry Tempest Williams, Aden Ross, Bill Ransom

Individual manuscript conferencing: yes

Enrollment: 50; *Enrollment limit:* 50

Ancillary activities: readings, Utah Shakespeare Festival, Methods of Teaching Writing seminars

WRITERS AT WORK CONFERENCE
P.O. Box 1146
Centerville, UT 84014-5146
tel: (801) 292-9285

A one-week conference with "workshops, afternoon panel discussions and lectures and access to other writers, editors and agents" and covering fiction (both long and short, and mystery), nonfiction, including essay, screenwriting and poetry.

Director/Contact: Writers at Work (nonprofit organization supporting creative writing in Utah)

Location(s): Park City, Utah

Dates: mid-July, 1996

Commenced: 1985

Recent faculty/lecturers: James Crumley, Dierdre McNamer, Dori Sanders,David Kranes, Linda M. Hasselstrom, Heather McHugh, Lee K. Abbott, Burton Hersh

Manuscript: required; *Individual manuscript conferencing:* yes; *Editing assistance:* yes; *Marketing guidance:* yes

Agents/editors attend: yes; *Available for conferencing:* yes

Enrollment: 300

Ancillary activities: fellowship competition and awards, readings, anthology

VERMONT

Bread Loaf Writers' Conference
Middlebury College
Middlebury, VT 05753-6111
tel: (802) 388-3711, ext. 5286

A two-week conference with daily lectures and workshops covering fiction, nonfiction, poetry and intensive manuscript critiques.

Director/Contact: Michael Collier, Director; Carol Knauss, Administrative Coordinator

Location(s): Mountain campus of Middlebury College, Ripton, VT

Dates: middle two weeks, August, 1996

Commenced: 1926

Recent faculty/lecturers: Donald Justice, Rosellen Brown, Nancy Willard, William Mathews, Julia Alvarez, Larry Brown, John Irving, Tim O'Brien

Manuscript: required; *Individual manuscript conferencing:* yes; *Marketing guidance:* yes

Agents/editors attend: yes; *Available for conferencing:* sometimes

Enrollment: 230; *Enrollment limit:* 230

Scholarships: yes

Ancillary activities: readings

Bennington Writing Workshops

Box BR
Bennington, VT 05201
tel: (802) 442-5401 ext 160
fax: (802) 442-6164

Two two-week workshop sessions in a program that "includes six hours of seminars per week, plus tutorial meetings with faculty and evening readings by visiting and resident writers. Many guest editors and publishers visit to participate in panel discussions." Covered are fiction, nonfiction and poetry.

Director/Contact: Liam Rector, Director; Priscilla Hodgkins, Assistant Director

Location(s): campus of Bennington College, Bennington, VT

Dates: July, 1996

Commenced: 1977

Recent faculty/lecturers: Lynn Freed, Barry Hannah, Elinor Lipman, Bob Shacochis, Stephen Dobyns, Molly Peacock, Douglas Bauer, Carole Maso, Sven Birkerts, Kate Daniels, Katha Pollitt, Kathleen Norris

Manuscripts: required; *Individual manuscript conferencing:* yes; *Editing assistance:* yes; *Marketing guidance:* yes

Agents/editors attend: yes; *Available for conferencing:* yes

Enrollment: 90 per session

Scholarships: yes

Ancillary activities: faculty and student readings

MEET... PRICILLA HODGKINS

ASSISTANT DIRECTOR,
BENNINGTON (VT) WRITING WORKSHOPS

I T WAS THE QUIET and serenity of Vermont that attracted
Priscilla Hodgkins after years in the business world in California.
Calling it her "mid-life time", she walked away from a lucrative job
that no longer fulfilled her and began a self-imposed "sabbatical"
which found her, months later, on the
campus of Bennington College in
Bennington, Vermont. "I came to the
Bennington campus out of curiosity," she
says. "I got fascinated with the scenery
and the college and ended up taking a job
as a secretary, so I could stay here."
Within a year she had become Assistant
Director of the Bennington Writing Workshops, working closely with Director Liam
Rector.

The Workshops began in 1977, an
idea of novelists John Gardner and Nicholas Del Bianco, both of
whom were faculty members at Bennington College. "It was a long
workshop—almost the entire month of July," says Hodgkins, noting
that no other workshops, then going, were as long. "But this would
give time to write and study," and, presumably, to develop solid, sub-
stantial work without deadline pressures.

From that moment the Bennington Writing Workshops have

always been in July, though it became apparent that a month-long session could not reach so many aspiring writers as two two-week sessions and that two weeks were more than sufficient to spark most students. Now, the Bennington Writing Workshops are firmly settled into two two-week sessions, "though each year," adds Hodgkins, "about 25 students stay on for both sessions."

As with most writers' get-togethers, everyone is broken into smaller groups. "We accept about 90 for each session, and we keep a ratio of 12 students to each workshop. We have workshops in fiction, poetry, nonfiction, and there are, usually, twice as many fiction workshops as poetry workshops and twice as many poetry workshops as nonfiction workshops." The workshops meet for two hours on Monday, Wednesday and Friday afternoons, and the students are encouraged to get together with their teachers at other, appropriate times. No one is required to write, "but the program is set up so people can write; we try to make it a very good place for that, so there's time to write while living in a community of writers."

"You just surround yourself in writing for two weeks," she emphasizes.

One thing is obvious about the Bennington program: it's not for the casual dabbler. "The criteria, here, is to be working on your writing. It's not a place for the hobbyist; it's a place for the serious student of writing." That seems clear when checking the roster of current and former faculty: Jill McCorkle, Barry Hannah, Stephan Dobyns, John Updike, Joyce Carol Oates, Jamaica Kincaid, Jayne Ann Phillips, among many others. "If someone is looking for a writers' workshop, 'How to Get Happily Published in 6 Hours or less,' don't come to Bennington," Hodgkins says. "That's just not going to happen here."

On the other hand, Hodgkins doesn't retreat behind a wall of literary one-upmanship when deciding who should come to the workshops. She helps review manuscript submissions, and there's no telling what will catch her eye. "A woman wanted to study nonfiction and sent copies of letters she sends to friends and relatives at holiday time. 'Oh no,' I thought, 'this won't work.' Then I began to read, and the letters were wonderful, absolutely wonderful, because of the detail, because of her control, because she could give us a whole scene, and it wasn't trivial. It reminded me of John O'Hara who could sum up a little society in a few words, and this woman, by telling about weddings and graduations and the little things that made up lives, did it with fine imagery and control.

Priscilla Hodgkins sees us—writers and readers—in a binding, synergistic partnership that will produce great rewards. "The exciting thing is that there are so many who have the need to write and so many who have the need to read. My end product is not only to make better writers, but to make better readers for each other, too."

DOROTHY CANFIELD FISHER WRITERS' CONFERENCE

P.O. Box 1058
Waitsfield, VT 05673-9710
tel: (802) 496-3271
fax: (802) 496-7271

A weekend conference with "twelve workshops for beginning to professional writers; from Writing 101 to contracts; from fiction how-to to nonfiction, and an editing workshop." Also included are workshops on writing for film and television, children's literature and marketing strategy.

Director/Contact: Kitty Werner, Director

Location(s) Sheraton-Burlington Hotel, Burlington, VT

Dates: 4th weekend in June, 1996

Commenced: 1990

Recent faculty/lecturers: Kirk Polking, Joseph Citro, William Noble, Kathy Saideman, Dawn Reno, Gayle Greeno

Individual manuscript conferencing: yes

Agents/editors attend: yes; *Available for conferencing:* yes

Enrollment: 100-120—no enrollment limit

Ancillary activities: bookfair, banquet

VERMONT STUDIO CENTER WRITER'S PROGRAM
P.O. Box 613
Johnson, VT 05656
tel: (802) 635-2727
fax: (802) 635-2730

This nonprofit organization "dedicated to supporting emerging and mid-career writers and visual artists offers two 2-week Writing Studio Sessions in fiction, creative nonfiction and poetry during February, March and April." In addition, a 2-week session in play writing is scheduled for 1996.

Director/Contact: Roger J. Kowalsky, Director

Locations(s): Johnson, VT

Dates: February, March, April, 1996

Commenced: 1993

Recent faculty/lecturers: Stephen Dobyns, Linda Gregg, Phillip Lopate, Grace Paley, William Mathews, Galway Kinnell, Musa Mayer, Lynne Sharson Schwartz

Manuscript required: yes; *Individual manuscript conferencing:* yes;

Enrollment: 72; *Enrollment limit:* 72: 12 per session/ 6 sessions

Scholarships: yes

Ancillary activities: readings

Wildbranch Workshop in Outdoor, Natural History and

Environmental Writing
Sterling College
Craftsbury Common, Vermont 05827
tel: (802) 586-7711
fax: (802) 586-2596

"A week-long workshop of classes, lectures, discussion groups and readings in the craft and techniques of fine writing about the world outdoors." Covered are fiction, nonfiction, essays, journalism, autobiographical writing.

Director/Contact: David W. Brown

Location (s): campus of Sterling College, Craftsbury Comon, VT

Dates: mid-late June, 1996

Commenced: 1988

Recent faculty: Michael Frome, John Hay, Robert Junco, Gale Lawrence, Steve Bodio, Ted Levin, Annie Proulx, George Wuerthner, Richard and Joyce Wolkomir

Individual manuscript conferencing: yes; *Editing assistance:* yes; *Marketing guidance:* yes

Agents/editors attend: editors only; *Available for conferencing:* yes

Enrollment: 25-30; *Enrollment limit:* 30

Scholarships: yes, a limited number

Ancillary activities: student and faculty readings, canoeing, fishing, bird watching, biking

VIRGINIA

CNU Writers' Conference

50 Shoe Lane
Newport News. VA 23606
tel: (804) 594-7158

A one-day conference sponsored by Christopher Newport College and offering workshops in six categories: fiction, nonfiction, poetry, children's literature, humor and publishing.

Director/Contact: Dr. Sue Jones, Director of Continuing Education

Location(s): campus of Christopher Newport College, Newport News, VA

Dates: first Saturday in April, 1996

Commenced: 1981

Recent faculty/lecturers: Dori Sanders, Joseph Bosco

Enrollment: 150

Ancillary activities: Writing contest for all categories with awards presentation in the evening; Celebration of the Arts, an informal social event, held Friday evening before conference with authors, artists musicians and conference registrants

Shenandoah Valley Writers' Guild
Lord Fairfax Community College
P.O. Box 47
Middletown, VA 22645
tel: (703) 869-1120

A one-day conference offering morning and afternoon workshops in popular genres (fiction, nonfiction, poetry, writing for children) and a keynote speaker.

Director/Contact: Felicia Cogan, Professor of English

Location(s): campus of Lord Fairfax Community College, Middletown, VA

Dates: May, 1996

Commenced: 1978

Editing assistance: yes; *Marketing guidance:* yes

Enrollment: 50

WASHINGTON

AMERICAN CHRISTIAN WRITERS CONFERENCE
(held March, 1996, Seattle, WA. See AZ for details)

CLARION WEST SCIENCE FICTION & FANTASY WRITERS WORKSHOP
340 15th Avenue E.
Suite 350
Seattle, WA 98112
tel: (206) 322-9083

This workshop is devoted to fiction only and is "an intensive six-week workshop for writers preparing for professional careers in science fiction and fantasy." Sponsored by a nonprofit literary organization, offering college credit with six full-time faculty members.

Director/Contact: Leslie Howle, Director

Location(s): campus of Seattle Central Community College, Seattle, WA

Dates: mid-June to end of July, 1996

Commenced: 1984

Recent faculty lecturers: Nancy Kress, Elizabeth Hand, Lucius Shepard, Gardner Dozois, John Crowley, Connie Willis, Joe Haldeman, Joan Vinge

Manuscript: required; *Individual manuscript conferencing:* yes; *Editing assistance:* yes; *Marketing guidance:* yes

Agents/editors attend: yes; *Available for conferencing:* yes

Enrollment: 20—"approximately 20 students will be selected"

Scholarships: yes—request the applicable form

Ancillary activities: readings

PACIFIC NORTHWEST WRITERS' CONFERENCE
2033 6th Avenue, Suite 804
Seattle, WA 98121
tel: (206) 443-3807
fax: (206) 441-8262

A three-day conference sponsored by a nonprofit literary organization "with morning to night panels and workshops appealing to published and aspiring writers in all categories from mystery and romance [as well as science fiction, women's fiction, children's literature] to nonfiction and poetry." Script writing and travel writing are also included.

Director/Contact: Shirley Bishop

Location(s): Seattle, WA area

Dates: third week, July, 1996

Commenced: 1945

Recent faculty/lecturers: Kathryn O. Galbraith, John Nichols, Mary Daheim, Colleen McElroy, Sharon Hashimoto, Jim Molnar

Individual manuscript conferencing: yes

Agents/editors attend: yes; *Available for conferencing:* yes

Enrollment: 700; *Enrollment limit:* 800

Ancillary activities: critique sessions, core groups, professional-advice panel, major literary contest, awards banquet, autograph party

PORT TOWNSEND WRITERS' CONFERENCE
Centrum Foundation
Box 1158
Port Townsend, WA 98368
tel: (360) 385-3102
fax: (360) 385-2470

A ten-day conference and series of workshops with "intense focus on serious fiction, poetry, essay writing and writing for children."

Director/Contact: Carol J. Bangs, PhD, Director

Location(s): Fort Worden State Park

Dates: middle ten days July, 1996

Commenced: 1973

Recent faculty/lecturers: Carolyn Kizer, Pam Houston, David Wagoner, Alan Cheuse, Valerie Miner, Richard Kenney, David Bradley, Marvin Bell, Pattiann Rogers, Jane Yolen

Manuscripts: required for workshops; *Individual manuscript conferencing:* yes; *Editing assistance:* yes

Agents/editors attend: yes

Enrollment: 160; *Enrollment limit:* 132 in workshops

Scholarships: yes

Ancillary activities: readings by faculty and guests, panels, display lectures, special-topic workshops, participant readings, social events

SEATTLE PACIFIC CHRISTIAN WRITERS' CONFERENCE

Seattle Pacific University
3rd West and Bertona
Seattle, WA 98119
tel: (206) 281-2109

A three-day conference with workshops, panels and motivational speakers for beginning-to-advanced writers of fiction, nonfiction, poetry, play writing and script writing.

Director/Contact: Linda Wagner

Location (s): campus of Seattle Pacific University, Seattle, WA

Dates: late June, 1996

Commenced: 1982

Recent faculty/lecturers: Walter Wangerin, Philip Yancy, Madeleine L'Engle

Individual manuscript conferencing: yes; *Editing assistance:* yes; *Marketing guidance:* yes

Agents/editors attend: yes; *Available for conferencing:* yes

Enrollment: 150-200—no enrollment limit

Scholarships: limited to missionaries home on leave or retired

Ancillary activities: readings

WRITE ON THE SOUND WRITERS' CONFERENCE
700 Main Street
Edmonds, WA 98020
tel: (206) 771-0228
fax: (206) 771-0253

A two-day conference sponsored by the Edmonds Arts Commision covering all aspects of writing: fiction (including specific genres such as romance, science fiction, mystery), nonfiction, poetry, writing for children, the business of writing, memoir writing.

Director/Contact: Christine Weed, Arts Coordinator

Location(s): Edmonds Library Plaza Room and Frances Anderson Center, Edmonds, WA

Dates: October 4-5, 1996

Commenced: 1985

Recent faculty/lecturers: Ann Rule, Jonathon Raban, Aaron Elkins, Tim Egan, Robert Ferigno, Margaret Chittended, Robert Ray, Irene Wanner, Ted and Gloria Rand

Individual manuscript conferencing: yes; *Editing assistance:* yes

Agents/editors attend: yes; *Available for conferencing:* yes

Enrollment: 160; *Enrollment limit:* 160

Ancillary activities: literary contest, manuscript critiques

WRITER'S WEEKEND AT THE BEACH
P.O. Box 877
Ocean Park, WA 98640
tel: (360) 665-6576

A weekend-long series of workshops for writers, photojournalists and poets covering fiction, nonfiction, poetry, play writing, children's literature.

Director/Contact: Birdie Etchison

Location(s): Ocean Park Methodist Retreat Center and Camp, Ocean Park, WA

Dates: February 23-25, 1996

Commenced: 1991

Recent faculty/lecturers: Peggy Anderson, Jan Bono, Gail Denham, Penny Lent, Patrica H. Rushford, Doyle Wesley Wells, Lauraine Snelling

Editing assistance: yes; *Marketing guidance:* yes

Enrollment: 50-55, including daily walk-ins

Ancillary activites: Saturday Evening Special (banquet)

WISCONSIN

GREAT LAKES WRITERS' WORKSHOP
Alverno College Telesis Institute
3401 S. 399th Street
P.O. Box 343922
Milwaukee, WI 53234-3922
tel: (414) 382-6177
fax: (414) 382-6354

One-week series of workshops for writers of all ability levels on varying writing topics, including fiction, poetry, nonfiction, children's literature, play writing.

Director/Contact: Debra Pass, Director, Telesis Institute

Location(s): campus of Alverno College, Milwaukee, WI

Dates: mid July, 1996

Commenced: 1984

Recent faculty/lecturers: William Nelson, Judy Bridges, Kathy Winkler

Editing assistance: yes; *Marketing guidance:* yes

Enrollment: 200; *Enrollment limit:* in certain workshops

GREEN LAKE WRITERS' CONFERENCE
American Baptist Assembly
W2511 State Highway 23
Green Lake, WI 54591-9300
tel: (414) 294-3323
fax: (414) 294-3848

A one-week conference with workshops, seminars and lectures in poetry, religious/inspirational writing, nonfiction and children's literature.

Director/Contact: Jan DeWitt

Location(s): Green Lake Conference Center, American Baptist Assembly, Green Lake, WI

Dates: July 13-20, 1996

Commenced: 1948

Recent faculty/lecturers: Lenore Colby, Dennis Hensley, Jeri McCormick, Sally Stuart, Gianfranco and Susan Pagnucci

Individual manuscript conferencing: yes; *Editing assistance:* yes; *Marketing guidance:* yes

Enrollment: 80

Scholarships: yes

Ancillary activities: the "Showcase" when many of the writings are shared

REDBIRD STUDIOS WRITERS' WORKSHOPS
3195 S. Superior Street
Milwaukee, WI 53207
tel: (414) 481-3027
fax: (414) 481-3027

Year-round workshops and seminars covering fiction (all genres), nonfiction, poetry, self publishing, journal writing, inspirational writing. Also provided is a performance component for those who are interested in acting, where the focus uses "monologues, short scenes and video feedback to teach script analysis, staging, movement and the development of character and voice."

Director/Contact: Judy Bridges

Location: Redbird Studios, local bed and breakfasts, campgrounds and private facilities in and around Milwaukee, WI

Dates: throughout 1996

Commenced: 1992

Recent faculty/lecturers: Elaine Bergstrom, Mary Ann O'Roarke, Patricia Lorenz, Chris Roerden

Editing assistance: yes; *Marketing guidance:* yes

Enrollment: 10-65

WISCONSIN REGIONAL WRITERS ASSOCIATION CONFERENCES

912 Cass Street
Portage, WI 53901
tel: (608) 742-24L0

A state-wide writer's organization (900-1000 members) offering two separate annual conferences covering fiction, nonfiction, poetry, essays, articles, short stories, humor, nostalgia, feature writing: a one-day conference in spring, a two day conference in fall.

Director/Contact: Elayne Clipper Hanson, President

Location(s): vary from year to year (1995 were Eau Claire and Stevens Point, WI)

Dates: May, September, 1996

Commenced: 1948

Recent faculty/lecturers: Marshall Cook, Jean Feraca, Marion Fuller Archer, Thomas Clark, Mary Conroy

Editing assistance: yes; ***Marketing guidance:*** yes

Agents/editors attend: yes

Enrollment: 125-150

Scholarships: yes, 3 provided annually to Rhinelander School of the Arts, Rhinelander, WI for one week in July

Ancillary activities: quarterly newsletter/magazine, bookfair, writing contests, "round" robin groups

CANADA

ARTSPERIENCE SUMMER SCHOOL OF THE ARTS
Canadore College
100 College Drive
North Bay, ON P1B 8K9
tel: (705) 474-7601
fax: (705) 494-7462

More than 70 workshops (one week–two weeks in length) offered during a one-month conference in many, varied crafts. Writing areas covered include fiction, nonfiction, poetry, play writing, film, television and video with classes throughout the day, Monday-Friday.

Director/Contact: Keith Campbell, Director

Location(s): campus of Canadore College, North Bay, ON

Dates: July 1-27, 1996

Commenced: 1978

Recent faculty/lecturers: Don Coles, Betty Jane Wylie, Robert Priest. C.H. (Marty) Gervais, Eugene McNamara, John B. Lee

Manuscript: required; *Individual manuscript conferencing:* yes; *Editing assistance:* yes; *Marketing guidance:* yes

Enrollment: 40-50 (in writing program), 800-900 total summer school participants; *Enrollment limit:* 10-16 per workshop class

Ancillary activities: readings open to the public, anthologies

CANADIAN AUTHOR'S ASSOCIATION ANNUAL CONFERENCE

275 Slater Street, Suite 500
Ottawa, ON, K1P 5H9
tel: (613) 233-2846
fax: (613) 235-8237

A five-day conference "bringing together writers, editors and publishers in a congenial atmosphere of seminars, workshops, panel discussion, readings by award-winning authors, and social events." Fiction, nonfiction, poetry, play writing, film, televison and video are covered.

Director/Contact: the National Office—hosting branch and conference coordinator changes each year

Location(s): Winnipeg, Manitoba

Dates: mid-June, 1996

Commenced: 1921

Recent faculty/lecturers: Edna Staebler, Arthur Black, Robert Munsch, Jacques G. Ruelland, Patrick Watson

Individual manuscript conferencing: yes; ***Marketing guidance:*** yes

Agents/editors attend: yes

Enrollment: 100-300

Ancillary activities: awards banquet, award-winner readings

MARITIME WRITERS' WORKSHOP
Dept. of Extension & Summer Session
University of New Brunswick
Box 4400
Fredericton, N.B.Canada, E3B 5A3
tel: (506) 454-4646
fax: (506) 453-3572

"Week-long workshops in fiction, nonfiction, poetry, writing for children, [and occasionally] play writing. Lectures, discussions, readings as well as daily workshop sessions."

Director/Contact: Glenda Turner, Coordinator

Location(s): University of New Brunswick, Fredericton, N.B., Canada

Dates: early July, 1996

Commenced: 1976

Recent faculty/lecturers: Elspeth Lamovan, Tim Wynne-Jones, Bill Gaston, Mia Anderson, Isabel Huggan

Manuscripts: required; *Individual manuscript conferencing:* yes; *Editing assistance:* yes; *Marketing guidance:* yes

Agents/editors attend: no

Enrollment: 50—5 workshops, l0 per class

Scholarships: yes; information sent to accepted applicants

Ancillary activities: a lecture each morning for full conference, readings each evening by instructors

Vancouver International Writers Festival

1243 Cartwright Street
Vancouver, B.C. V6H 4B7
tel: (604) 681-6330
fax: (604) 681-8400

A five-day festival that attracts more than 8000 people, "presenting Canadian and International writers and providing them with an often rare opportunity to interact with each other and with the audience." There are readings and discussions on fiction, nonfiction, poetry, children's literature, genre writing. Attendance is through ticket purchase.

Director/Contact: Alma Lee, Producer

Location (s): Granville Island, Vancouver, B.C.

Dates: mid-October, 1996

Commenced: 1988

Recent faculty/lecturers: Maeve Binchy, Martha Brooks, George Bowering, Roch Carrier, Robertson Davies, Diana Gabaldon, Barry Lopez

Ancillary activities: The Bill Duthie Memorial Lecture

Writing From the Edge

Atlin Art Center
Monarch Mountain, B.C. V0W 1A0
tel: (604) 651-7659
(416) 536-7971
fax: (604) 651-7659

A 2-week workshop "which invites an attitude of creative play [where] every experience can become a source of personal expression." Fiction, nonfiction and poetry are covered and the emphasis is on "writing through experiencing."

Director/Contact: Gernot Dick, Director

Dates: August, 1996

Commenced: new program

Faculty/lecturers: Marilyn Walker, Gernot Dick, Cate Collie

Enrollment: 20; *Enrollment limit:* 20

SUPPLEMENTAL LIST

S OME WRITERS' CONFERENCES and workshops did not re-
spond to requests for information, but the most significant of
them can't be ignored in a volume which calls itself a Complete
Guide. The following is a winnowed list of conferences and
workshops that, in the past, have offered major programs in areas of
fiction, nonfiction and poetry. Deliberately excluded are narrowly fo-
cussed or one-specialty programs, those which have little or no track
record and those which have space for only a handful of students.
Arrangement here is alphabetical by state:

MIDNIGHT SUN WRITERS'
CONFERENCE
University of Alaska Fairbanks
Fairbanks, AK 00775
att: Frank Soos, English Department

SOCIETY OF SOUTHWESTERN
AUTHORS
Annual Writers' Conference
P.O. Box 30355
Tuscon, AZ 85751-0355
att: Don Young

BAY AREA WRITERS' WORKSHOP
1450 Fourth Street #4
Berkeley, CA 94710
att: Joyce Jenkins, Director

CALIFORNIA WRITERS' CLUB
CONFERENCE
2214 Derby Street
Berkeley, CA 94705
att: Dorothy Benson, Secretary

INTERNATIONAL BLACK
WRITERS AND ARTISTS INC.
CONFERENCE
Local 1
Box 43576
Los Angeles, CA 90043

JACK LONDON WRITERS'
CONFERENCE
222 Avey Avenue
Menlo Park, CA 94025
att: Barbara Foley

NAPA VALLEY WRITERS'
CONFERENCE
Napa Valley College
2277 Napa-Vallejo Highway
Napa, CA 94558
att: Sherri Hallgren

SIERRA NEVADA WRITING
INSTITUTE
(held in California)
University of Nevada
Reno, NV 89557
att: Stephan Tchudi

SOUTHERN CALIFORNIA WRITERS' CONFERENCE
2596 Escondido Avenue
San Diego, CA 92123
att: Barbara Hartner Sack

WEST MARIN WRITERS' CONFERENCE
Suite 201
#1 Weatherly Drive
Mill Valley, CA 94941
att: Peter Robinson

WRITE TO SELL WRITERS' CONFERENCE
8465 Jane Street
San Diego, CA 92129
att: Diane Dunaway

ASPEN WRITERS' CONFERENCE
Drawer 7726
Aspen, CO 81612
att: Karen Chamberlain

FLORIDA WRITERS IN TOUCH FORIDA CHRISTIAN WRITERS' CONFERENCE
2600 Park Avenue
Titusville, FL 32780
att: Billie Wilson, Director

SUNCOAST WRITERS' CONFERENCE
University of South Florida
4202 E. Fowler Avenue
Tampa, FL 33620
att: Gianna Russo, English
Department

EMORY SUMMER WRITERS' INSTITUTE
c/o English Department
Emory University
Atlanta, GA 30322
att: Sally Wolff, Assistant Dean

SANDHILLS WRITERS' CONFERENCE
Augusta College
2500 Walton Way
Augusta, GA 30910
att: Theresa Bryant, Director

BLOOMING GROVE WRITERS' CONFERENCE
Box 515
Bloomington, IL 61702
att: Bettie Story

THE WORLD OF FREELANCE WRITING
College of DuPage
22nd and Lambert Roads
Glen Ellyn, IL 60137
att: Sara Weinstein

PRAIRIE SUMMER WRITERS' CONFERENCE
Prairie Writers' Group
201 S. Highland
Fairfield, IA 52556
att: Meg Fitz-Randolph

APPALACHIAN WRITERS' WORKSHOP
Hindman Settlement School
Hindman, KY 41822
att: Mike Mullins

CREATIVE WRITING CONFERENCE
Eastern Kentucky University
Richmond, KY 40475
att: Dorothy Sutton

WOMEN WRITERS' CONFERENCE
University of Kentucky
208 Patterson Office Tower
Lexington, KY 40506-0277
att: Jan Oaks

NEW ORLEANS WRITERS' CONFERENCE
University of New Orleans
Office of Conference Services
New Orleans, LA 70148

MAINE WRITERS' AND PUBLISHERS' ALLIANCE
The Maine Writer's Center
12 Pleasant Street
Brunswick, ME 04011

STONECOAST WRITERS' CONFERENCE
University of Southern Maine
    Extension
96 Falmouth Street
Portland, ME 04103
att: Barbara Hope

THE ART OF NONFICTION CONFERENCE
39 Trellium Way
Amherst, MA 01002
att: Madeleine Blais, Director

CAPE COD WRITERS' CONFERENCE
Cape Cod Conservatory
Route 132
W. Barnstable, MA 02688
att: Marion Vuilleumier, Director

GARY PROVOST'S WRITERS' WORKSHOP
Box 139
S. Lancaster, MA 01561
att: Gail/Gary Provost

EASTERN WRITERS' CONFERENCE
English Department
Salem State College
Salem, MA 01970
att: Rod Kessler, Director

HARVARD SUMMER WRITING PROGRAM
51 Brattle Street
Cambridge, MA 02138
att: David S. Gewanter

MARTHA'S VINYARD WRITERS' WORKSHOP
The Nathan Mayhew Seminars
P.O. Box 1125
Vinyard Haven, MA 02568
att: Patty Blakesley

THIRD COAST WRITERS' CONFERENCE
English Department
Western Michigan University
Kalamazoo, MI 49008-5092
att: Tamara Skidmore

WESTERN MONTANA WRITERS' CONFERENCE
Summer School Office
Western Montana College
Dillon, MT 59725
att: Sue Jones

YELLOW BAY WRITERS' CONFERENCE
Center for Continuing Education
University of Montana
Missoula, MT 59812
att: Judy Jones, Director

NEBRASKA WRITERS' GUILD
Fall & Spring Conferences
14824 Parker Plaza
Omaha, NB 68154
att: Shirly Maly, Program Director

WRITING BY THE SEA
Cape May Institute Inc.
1511 New York Avenue
Cape May, NJ 08210
att: Natalie Newton, Managing
    Director

SANTA FE WRITERS'
 CONFERENCE
826 Camino de Monte Rey
Suite A-3Santa Fe, NM 87001
att: Julie Shigekuni, Director

CATSKILL POETRY WORKSHOP
c/o Special Program Office
Hartwick College
Oneonta, NY 13820
att: Carol Frost, Director

CHAUTAUQUA WRITERS'
 WORKSHOP
Box 109B
Chautauqua, NY 14722
att: Jack Voelker

INTERNATIONAL WOMENS'
 WRITING GUILD
P.O. Box 810
Gracie Station, NY 10028
att: Hannelore Hahn, Director

MARYMOUNT MANHATTAN
 WRITERS' CONFERENCE
Marymount Manhattan College
221 E. 71st Street
New York, NY 10021

SARAH LAWRENCE SUMMER
 SESSION FOR WRITERS
1 Mead Way
Bronxville, NY 10708-5999
att: Susan Guma

WRITE ASSOCIATES WRITERS'
 CONFERENCE
471 Burroughs
Buffalo, NY 14266
att: Janet Vine, Registrar

WRITERS ON WRITING AT
 BARNARD
Barnard College
3009 Broadway
New York, NY 10027-6598
att: Ann Birnstein

BLUE RIDGE CHRISTIAN
 WRITERS' CONFERENCE
P.O. Box 188
Black Mountain, NC 26711
att: Yvonne Lehman, Director

WILDERNESS WRITERS'
 WORKSHOP
233 S. Elm Street
Greesboro, NC 27401
att: Judith Hill, Director

ANTIOCH WRITERS' WORKSHOP
Box 494
Yellow Springs, OH 45387
att: Susan Carpenter

CUYAHOGA WRITERS'
 CONFERENCE
Cuyahoga Community College
4250 Richmond Road
Highland Hills Village, OH 44122
att: Margo Bohanon

SINCLAIR COMMUNITY
 COLLEGE WRITERS' CONF.
444 W. Third Street
Dayton, OH 45402

WILLAMETTE WRITERS'
 CONFERENCE
9045 S.W. Barbur Blvd, #5A
Portland, OR 97219
att: Linda Stirling Wanner

LIGONIER VALLEY WRITERS'
CONFERENCE
Box 8, RR 4
Ligonier, PA 15658
att: Tina Thoburn

PHILADELPHIA WRITERS'
CONFERENCE
P.O. Box 7171
Philadelphia, PA 19117
att: Gloria Delaman

FRANCIS MARION WRITERS'
CONFERENCE
English Department
Francis Marion College
Florence, SC 29501
att: David Starkey

AUSTIN WRITER'S LEAGUE
WORKSHOP
Suite E-2
15001 W. 5th Street
Austin, TX 78703
att: Angela Smith

FRONTIERS IN WRITING
CONFERENCE
Panhandle Professional Writers
P.O. Box 19303
Amarillo, TX 79114
att: Doris Meredith, President

DESERT WRITERS' CONFERENCE
P.O. Box 68
Moab UT 84532
att: Canyon Fields Institute

BLUE RIDGE WRITERS'
CONFERENCE
Center For Community Education
Roanoke College
Salem, VA 24153

CHESAPEAKE WRITERS'
CONFERENCE
Rappahannock Community College
Glenns, VA 23149
att: Jane Deringer/ Rick Ughetto

CANADA

OTTAWA INDEPENDENT
WRITERS' CONFERENCE
Room 302, Administration Building
Carleton, University
Ottawa, ON K1S 5B6

SASKATCHEWAN WRITERS'
GUILD CONFERENCE
Box 3986
Regina, Saskatchewan S4P 3R9

WRITERS' WORKSHOP
University of Toronto
158 St. George Street
Toronto, ON M5S 2V8

INDEXES

MONTH OR SEASON

The following conferences and workshops are held at various times during at least one season of the year:

SPECIALTY/GENRE

FICTION

NONFICTION

SCHOLARSHIPS/ DISCOUNTS

WRITING CONTESTS

General Index